THE THRIVE ADHD SUCCESS FORMULA

TRANSFORM DISTRACTION INTO FOCUS, TURN CHALLENGES INTO STRENGTHS, AND MANAGE EMOTIONS WITH ADULTS' ADHD GUIDE

A.W. HIYASAT

CONTENTS

INTRODUCTION

I stared at the same paragraph for what felt like the hundredth time, the words swimming before my eyes as my mind drifted to everything except the CPA exam materials in front of me. The clock showed another hour had somehow vanished. The familiar wave of panic and self-doubt crashed over me: "What do you think you're doing? You're just wasting your time. People like you don't pass exams like this." As the negative thoughts spiraled, I wondered how I'd ever make it through graduate school when I couldn't even focus on a single chapter.

Time races. your brain stalls

This wasn't a new feeling. I'd spent years battling my brain, trying to force it into submission. Sticky notes covered my desk, my walls, and even my bathroom mirror. I had downloaded every productivity app, tried every study technique, and still found myself staring at the clock at 2 a.m., wondering where the day had gone and why I had so little to show for it.

"Just focus harder." That's what everyone told me. As if I hadn't been trying to do exactly that my entire life. "Find a quiet place without distractions." I tried libraries, empty classrooms, and even a closet once. Nothing worked. My mind would find distractions in empty space: counting ceiling tiles, making patterns out of wood grain, or spiraling into elaborate daydreams about what I'd do after passing this exam that I couldn't seem to study for.

I didn't know then that my brain was wired differently. That the constant struggle wasn't a character flaw but a neurological reality. That my difficulty sitting still, staying on task, and managing time wasn't laziness or a lack of willpower; it was undiagnosed ADHD.

The diagnosis came during my second semester of graduate school. I'd somehow made it through undergrad with decent grades, a combination of last-minute panic-fueled all-nighters, generous professors, and subjects that naturally captured my interest. But the CPA exam and graduate-level accounting classes were different beasts entirely. Detail-oriented, rule-based, requiring sustained focus for hours on end; they were practically designed to expose every weakness of my ADHD brain.

When the doctor said "adult ADHD," I felt a rush of emotions. Relief, yeah, there was a name for this thing I'd been fighting my whole life. But also doubt. Wasn't ADHD just for hyperactive kids? Wasn't I too successful to have a "disorder"? I had a bachelor's degree and a job, after all. And underneath it all, fear, what now? Would medication make me a different person? Was I just looking for an excuse?

But mostly, I felt stuck. The diagnosis explained a lot, but it didn't immediately solve anything. The CPA exam deadline wasn't going anywhere. Graduate school assignments still piled up. Life didn't pause while I figured out what having ADHD meant.

I tried the standard advice. Medication helped, but it wasn't a magic fix; it created space for better focus, but didn't tell me how to use that space. Traditional study advice still failed me. "Study in complete silence" left me climbing the walls after twenty minutes. "Eliminate all distractions" was impossible when my own thoughts were the biggest distraction. "Make a detailed study schedule" became just another piece of paper I'd lose or ignore when my brain decided that reorganizing my sock drawer was suddenly the most urgent task in the universe.

So, I started experimenting. Getting curious about what actually worked for my brain rather than fighting against it. And what I discovered surprised me.

I noticed something weird: Having reruns of shows I'd seen a million times playing quietly in the background actually helped me focus better than silence. Shows like *Friends* or *The Office*—stuff I'd watched so many times I could recite the dialogue—gave my fidgety brain just enough background noise to stay satisfied while the rest of me worked on studying. It made no sense, but it worked.

Breaking things down helped, too. Trying to study for three hours straight? Disaster. But telling myself, "Just do 25 minutes, then you can get up and stretch"? That, I could handle. Doodling during lectures kept me present instead of zoning out completely. Explaining concepts aloud to my empty room somehow made the information stick when silent reading failed me.

The biggest thing was tiny goals with instant payoffs. Forget "finish this chapter tonight," that was a recipe for doing nothing. Instead, I'd tell myself, "Just ten practice questions, then you can check Instagram for five minutes." Ten questions felt possible. And that little break was enough to keep me going for another round after.

None of this came from study guides or advice columns. It came from paying attention to when I actually got stuff done versus when I spun my wheels. From being honest about how my brain worked instead of how I wished it worked. From stopping the constant self-punishment for not being able to focus "normally."

Bit by bit, things got better. One chapter became two. A handful of practice questions turned into dozens. My test scores started climbing. The knot of anxiety that had lived in my stomach for years began to loosen as I realized I could work with my weird brain instead of constantly fighting it.

Bad days? Yeah, plenty of those still. Days when I'd read the same paragraph over and over, comprehending nothing. Days when I'd snap back to reality and realize I'd spent an hour researching something completely unrelated to what I was supposed to be studying. But these weren't total disasters anymore. I had workarounds. Ways to get myself back on track when things went sideways.

Six months after diagnosis, I passed the first section of the CPA exam. After passing that first section, I completed another section every two to three months. It took longer than I had planned, but I came to understand that putting intense time pressure on an ADHD brain often works against it. I finished my master's degree without the constant crisis mode I'd been operating in for years. When I went back to managing the metal fabrication shop, I brought these new approaches with me, transforming how I handled the mountains of paperwork and planning that had always been my nemesis.

The real change wasn't just having better tricks for studying or working. It was how I thought about my brain. I stopped seeing ADHD as this terrible defect. Started seeing it more like, I don't know, like having a quirky old car instead of a new sedan. Yeah, it's got its problems; sometimes it won't start, but it also has some things going for it that other cars don't. My ability to hyperfocus on interesting problems, to see connections nobody else noticed, and to bring energy and enthusiasm when I was engaged: These weren't separate from my ADHD. They came with the territory.

This changed everything. Instead of constantly fighting my nature, I started working with it. Instead of seeing myself as fundamentally broken, I saw myself as differently equipped. Instead of obsessing over what I couldn't do, I started leveraging what I could.

But my journey didn't stop there. What makes my experience unique is that I've tested my ADHD to its absolute limit, beyond the edge, to the point of falling off the cliff. That became the ultimate test: pushing my brain past its breaking point, then rebuilding it piece by piece. When the mind was put back together, I began testing its performance again, this time with intention, awareness, and respect for how it works.

The same person who once struggled to read a single book is now writing one. The person who fought through every page of a master's degree is now pursuing a PhD, not just reading and absorbing information, but producing dense, complex academic papers and dissertations. I've gone from barely being able to focus on words to building structured arguments supported by research and evidence.

And that's what this book is really about. Not "curing" ADHD or forcing your brain to behave like everyone else's. It's about understanding your particular version of ADHD and finding practical ways to work with your natural tendencies instead of against them. It's about turning what feels like your biggest weakness into something that might actually help you stand out. And it's about showing that transformation is possible, even when the odds seem stacked against you. This isn't just about mastering techniques or following a specific system. It's about showing that there are ways forward, even if they're different for each of us.

In the coming chapters, I'll get into the specifics of what worked for me. We'll start with the mindset stuff, how reframing ADHD changes everything else. Then we'll dig into concrete strategies for finding focus when your attention naturally bounces all over the place. We'll tackle time management when you basically can't feel time passing. We'll look at handling the emotional ups and downs.

We'll also get practical about applying these approaches at work and in relationships, places where ADHD challenges often cause the most grief. And we'll work on building all these individual tactics into something sustainable.

The THRIVE ADHD Success Formula

The chapters in this book follow a framework I built specifically for how ADHD brains work: THRIVE.

THRIVE breaks down the core pillars of ADHD success into six pieces:

- **T** → **Tame Your Thoughts (Chapter 1)** is where we start, because how you think about your ADHD shapes everything else. This is about stopping the "I'm lazy" or "I'm broken" narrative and recognizing ADHD for what it actually is: a neurological difference. Getting this right makes everything else easier.

- **H** → **Harness Your Attention (Chapter 2)** gives you practical ways to work with your brain's attention patterns instead of fighting them. You'll learn how to set up environments and use tools that help you focus when it counts.

- **R** → **Regulate Your Time (Chapter 3)** tackles the time-blindness problem. Your brain doesn't naturally track time the way other people do, so we'll build external systems that make time something you can actually see and manage.

- **I** → **Integrate Your Emotions (Chapter 4)** is here because ADHD isn't just about focus and time; it's also about feeling everything intensely. You'll get strategies for working with big emotions instead of being steamrolled by them.

- **V** → **Value Your Strengths (Chapters 5 and 6)** flips the script from what's hard about ADHD to what's powerful about it. We'll look at how to use your natural strengths at work, in relationships, and when designing a life that actually fits you.

- **E** → **Engage Your Support (Chapter 7)** accepts a simple truth: You're not supposed to do this alone. We'll put together your tool kit of resources, systems, people, and professional help that let your brain work at its best.

You don't have to do everything at once or read straight through. Some people start with mindset (T) and work through in order. Others jump straight to whatever's killing them right now—focus (H), time (R), emotions (I), work stuff or relationship issues (V), or getting help (E)—and come back to the rest later. Use it however makes sense for you.

Look, I know you've probably tried a bunch of approaches already. Maybe you've read other ADHD books that gave you cookie-cutter advice that didn't stick. Maybe you've beaten yourself up for not being able to follow strategies that seem to work fine for everyone else. Maybe you're skeptical that anything is really going to help.

I get that. I've been exactly where you are, wondering if things would ever get easier. The difference with what I'm sharing isn't that it's some revolutionary new science; it's that it comes from someone who's been in the trenches with this stuff. These aren't strategies I read about in a psychology journal; they're approaches I cobbled together through desperate trial and error while my academic and professional future hung in the balance.

Will everything be smooth sailing from here? Nope. There will still be days that kick your butt. But I can tell you this: With approaches that actually match how your brain is wired, things really can improve. Dramatically. That same brain that fights you every step of the way with traditional methods can become surprisingly effective when you give it the right environment and tools.

If nothing else, I want you to walk away from this book knowing this: You're not stranded. There's always a way to rebuild. There's always a solution waiting to be found, and if someone else has found theirs, you can find yours, too.

So, if you're tired of fighting your brain and ready to try working with it instead, keep reading. The path forward isn't about becoming someone else; it's about becoming a better version of who you already are.

CHAPTER 1

TAME
YOUR
THOUGHTS

REFRAMING ADHD FROM
DISORDER TO DYNAMIC TRAIT

My whole life, I thought I was broken. Not in a dramatic way that anyone could see from the outside, but in a quiet, persistent way that colored everything I did. Why couldn't I just sit down and focus like everyone else? Why did my mind constantly bounce from thought to thought like a pinball? Why was I always losing things, running late, and struggling to finish what I started?

After my ADHD diagnosis, my first instinct was to think of it as confirmation of that brokenness. I had a disorder. A deficit. My brain wasn't working properly. Even the name—attention deficit hyperactivity disorder—screamed that something was missing, that I was somehow less than.

But the more I learned about ADHD, the more I realized how wrong that thinking was. I wasn't broken; I was different. My brain wasn't deficient; it was wired in a way that made certain things harder and other things easier. This realization didn't happen overnight. It came in fits and starts, in small epiphanies and gradual shifts in how I thought about myself.

It began with a simple question from my therapist: "What if your ADHD brain isn't broken, just different?"

This chapter builds the "T" pillar of the *THRIVE ADHD Success Formula*. Before you can harness your attention, manage your time, or regulate your emotions, you need to shift how you think about your ADHD itself. This pillar is about reframing ADHD from a personal failing into a neurological difference, moving from shame to curiosity, and understanding that your "broken" brain is actually just wired differently.

Understanding ADHD as Different Brain Wiring

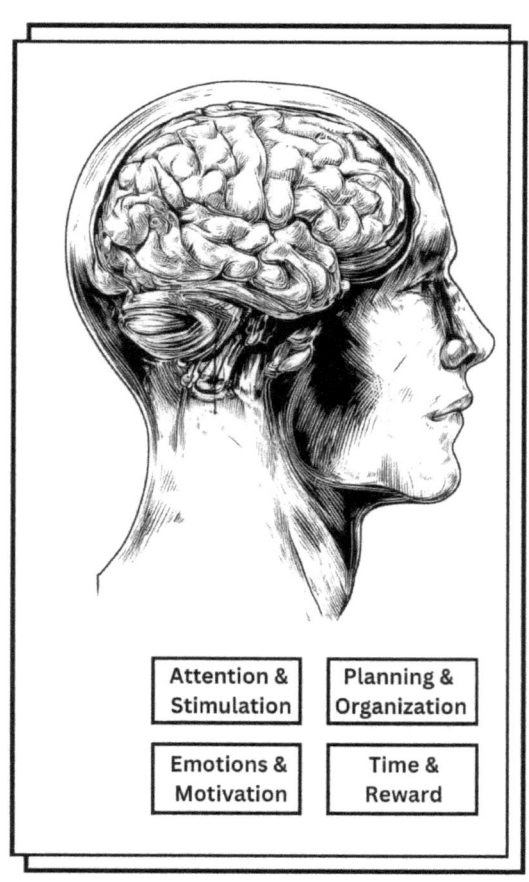

Let's talk about what's actually happening in an ADHD brain. Not the medical jargon or the clinical criteria, the real, biological differences that explain why our experience of the world is so different from someone without ADHD.

The simplest way to understand it is this: The ADHD brain processes dopamine differently than the neurotypical brain. Dopamine is that feel-good chemical that helps us feel motivated, focused, and rewarded. In ADHD brains, dopamine doesn't hang around long enough to do its job properly. It's like trying to fill a bathtub when someone keeps pulling the plug; the water (dopamine) drains out too quickly to reach the level needed.

This isn't a minor issue. Dopamine affects everything from how we experience rewards to how we maintain attention to how we regulate our emotions. When dopamine doesn't work the way it's supposed to, it creates a cascade of effects that shape how we interact with the world.

Think about a time when you were completely absorbed in something you loved: maybe a video game, an interesting conversation, or a creative project. You lost track of time. You didn't want to stop. Everything else faded into the background. That's your dopamine system working at full throttle. For people with ADHD, that system tends to underperform with everyday tasks but can kick into high gear with the right triggers, usually things that are novel, challenging, interesting, or urgent.

It's not just dopamine, either. Several areas of the brain tend to develop and function differently in people with ADHD. The prefrontal cortex, which handles executive functions like planning, organization, and impulse control, shows different patterns of activity. The connections between different brain regions can be less robust. The default mode network, which is active when we're daydreaming or lost in thought, can be harder to switch off when it's time to focus.

These aren't deficits; they're differences. And they explain so much about the ADHD experience that gets misinterpreted as character flaws.

When I couldn't make myself study for the CPA exam despite desperately wanting to pass, it wasn't because I was lazy; it was because my brain's reward system wasn't registering future benefits as strongly as immediate ones. When I'd blurt out thoughts in the middle of meetings at the fabrication shop, it wasn't because I was rude; it was because my impulse control systems needed extra support. When I'd lose track of time and show up late, it wasn't because I was disrespectful; it was because my brain processed time differently.

Understanding these neurological differences was incredibly freeing. After years of beating myself up, of thinking I just needed more willpower or discipline, I finally realized I was trying to force my brain to work in ways it simply wasn't designed to work. It was like trying to drive a speedboat down a highway, no wonder I was struggling!

The turning point came when I stopped seeing ADHD as something wrong with me and started seeing it as just a different kind of brain. Some neuroscientists and psychologists call this idea "neurodiversity"; the concept that different types of brain wiring aren't defective, just different, and that this diversity serves important evolutionary and social purposes.

Think about it this way: In prehistoric times, having some members of the tribe who were constantly scanning the environment for changes or who could hyperfocus on tracking an animal would be incredibly valuable. Even today, different brain types bring different strengths to the table. Some situations require focused, methodical thinking. Others benefit from quick, flexible thinking and creative connections, exactly what the ADHD brain excels at.

This shift in perspective changed everything for me. Instead of fighting against my nature, I could start working with it. Instead of trying to become someone I wasn't, I could learn to become the best version of who I actually am.

I remember sitting in a coffee shop, studying for the audit section of the CPA exam. Previously, I'd have forced myself to sit perfectly still, to focus only on the textbook, to eliminate all "distractions." And I'd inevitably fail, ending up frustrated and feeling like a failure.

But this day was different. I had my textbook, yes, but also my fidget cube that I could manipulate under the table. I had instrumental music playing through my headphones. I'd broken my study session into 25-minute chunks with rewards built in. And most importantly, I'd let go of the shame. When my mind wandered, which it still did, I gently brought it back without the usual self-criticism.

That day, I studied for four hours and actually retained what I learned. It wasn't because my ADHD had magically disappeared. It was because I'd stopped trying to study like someone without ADHD and started working with my brain's natural tendencies instead of against them.

The Science Behind ADHD Strengths

Here's something they don't tell you when you get diagnosed: ADHD doesn't just come with challenges; it comes with strengths. Real, measurable, valuable strengths that are directly connected to the same brain differences that create the challenges.

Creativity

Let's talk about creativity first. People with ADHD often show greater divergent thinking: the ability to generate multiple ideas and think outside conventional patterns. There's actually a neurological basis for this. Because our brains have less robust filtering mechanisms, we make connections between ideas that others might filter out as irrelevant. What looks like "random" thinking to others can actually be the foundation of innovation and problem-solving.

I saw this firsthand in the metal fabrication shop. When equipment broke down or a customer needed something unusual, I could quickly generate multiple solutions, considering possibilities that others dismissed. While my colleagues would methodically work through the standard troubleshooting steps, my mind would leap to connections and possibilities they hadn't considered. This wasn't despite my ADHD; it was because of it.

Hyperfocus

Then there's hyperfocus, that almost magical ability to become completely absorbed in tasks that capture our interest. Neurologically, this happens when something sufficiently engages our brain's reward system, creating a flood of dopamine that allows sustained attention and information processing. While we struggle to focus on boring tasks, we can focus with unusual intensity on engaging ones.

During my CPA exam preparation, I discovered I could hyperfocus on practice exams; the immediate feedback and challenge kept my brain engaged, even though reading textbooks was torture. At work, I could lose myself for hours in solving complex logistical problems or designing more efficient workshop layouts, completely losing track of time and surroundings.

Resilience

Resilience is another common ADHD strength, though it's rarely discussed. People with ADHD often develop extraordinary determination and adaptability from years of navigating a world not designed for their brains. We learn to bounce back from setbacks because we've had so much practice at it. We develop creative workarounds because the standard approaches often don't work for us.

Dr. Edward Hallowell, one of the leading experts on ADHD and someone who has it himself, puts it this way: "One of the most powerful steps for people with ADHD is recognizing what a positive attribute ADHD can be and actively looking for its upsides." He describes ADHD not as a disorder but as a "trait" that comes with both challenges and advantages (Hallowell, 2020).

Understanding these strengths completely transformed my relationship with ADHD. Instead of seeing only what I couldn't do, I began to appreciate what I could do differently, and sometimes better, than others. This wasn't about denying the real challenges of ADHD. It was about seeing the complete picture instead of focusing only on the difficulties.

This reframing allowed me to work with my nature rather than against it. I stopped trying to force myself into approaches that consistently failed me and started leveraging my natural tendencies. High energy became an asset when channeled properly. Curiosity and quick thinking became professional strengths rather than distractions to suppress. Even my tendency to get bored quickly pushed me to create more efficient systems so I could move on to more interesting tasks.

Masking   Being Yourself

Challenging Common Misconceptions

Let's be honest; there's a lot of BS out there about ADHD. Misconceptions that not only mislead others but that we ourselves often internalize, adding layers of shame on top of our actual challenges. Let's take these myths apart one by one.

1. **"ADHD is just an excuse for laziness."** This one cut deep for me because I'd believed it about myself for years. But ADHD isn't about lack of effort; it's about inconsistent access to mental resources that others take for granted.

The ADHD brain can work incredibly hard but struggles to direct that effort consistently, especially toward tasks that don't engage our dopamine system.

I wasn't lazy when I spent twelve hours trying to force myself to study, even if I only managed to focus for three of those hours. I wasn't lazy when I tried every productivity system I could find, desperately looking for something that would work for my brain. I was working twice as hard as my classmates for half the results: the opposite of laziness.

2. **"Adults outgrow ADHD."** This persistent myth left me believing something was extra wrong with me since I still struggled as an adult. The reality? About 60-70% of children with ADHD continue to have significant symptoms into adulthood (Adesman, 2001). The way ADHD presents may change; hyperactivity often becomes more internal, like racing thoughts or restlessness, but the underlying brain differences remain.

3. **"ADHD only affects academic performance."** If only! ADHD impacts every area of life: relationships, work, emotional regulation, self-care, finances, driving, you name it. It's not just about having trouble reading textbooks or sitting through lectures.

In my case, ADHD affected how I managed the fabrication shop, how I maintained friendships, how I handled my finances, and even how I approached hobbies and interests. Recognizing this broader impact was crucial for developing effective strategies that addressed my whole life, not just academic or work performance.

1. **"People with ADHD just need to try harder."** This toxic myth assumes the problem is effort rather than brain wiring. It's like telling someone with nearsightedness to "try harder" to see the blackboard instead of getting them glasses. ADHD isn't about effort; it's about access to consistent executive function, which is largely controlled by brain chemistry and structure, not willpower.

2. **"ADHD is overdiagnosed/not real/invented by pharmaceutical companies."** Despite overwhelming scientific evidence—brain imaging studies, genetic research, longitudinal studies following children into adulthood—these myths persist. ADHD is one of the most well-researched conditions in psychiatry, with evidence for its biological basis dating back decades.

Before I understood my ADHD, I internalized many of these misconceptions. Each time I struggled with something that seemed easy for others, a voice in my head would whisper, "You're just lazy. You just don't care enough. You're just making excuses." These thoughts became a constant background soundtrack, eroding my self-esteem and adding emotional suffering on top of the practical challenges.

Learning that ADHD comes with incredible upsides, including creativity, hyperfocus, and energy when viewed in a positive light, didn't just change how I managed my symptoms; it transformed how I viewed myself. I wasn't broken or defective. I had a brain that worked differently, with both challenges and strengths.

Mindset as the First Step to Success

Here's what I've learned: Your beliefs about your ADHD fundamentally shape your experience of it. If you see ADHD solely as a deficit, something wrong with you that limits what you can achieve, you'll focus on what you can't do and overlook potential strengths. But if you see ADHD as a different brain wiring with both challenges and advantages, you open up possibilities for working with your nature rather than constantly fighting against it.

This isn't just positive thinking or wishful psychology. Research on what psychologists call "mindset" shows that how we think about our traits and abilities deeply affects our outcomes (Parsamanesh & Vysochyn, 2024). People with a fixed mindset believe their traits are unchangeable, while those with a growth mindset believe they can develop their abilities through effort and strategy.

When it comes to ADHD, a growth mindset doesn't mean you can eliminate your ADHD through sheer effort. It means recognizing that while your brain wiring may be relatively fixed, your strategies, environments, and the impact of ADHD on your life aren't. You can learn, adapt, and develop approaches that work with your brain rather than against it.

This mindset shift was the foundation for everything else in my journey. Once I accepted that passing the CPA exam, completing my master's degree, and succeeding at work would require different approaches for my ADHD brain, not just more effort within traditional frameworks, I could start finding solutions that actually worked.

Here's a simple example: I used to see my distractibility purely as a weakness. When I'd notice something in my environment that others missed, a subtle change in someone's expression during a meeting, an unusual sound from a piece of machinery, a pattern in sales data that wasn't obvious to others, I'd scold myself for not staying "on task."

But with a shifted mindset, I began to recognize this heightened environmental awareness as potentially valuable. In meetings, I started noticing interpersonal dynamics that others missed. In the fabrication shop, I'd catch early signs of equipment problems because some small change in sound or vibration caught my attention. What had been a "deficit" in attention could actually be an asset in the right context.

Similarly, I'd always seen my tendency to get bored with routine tasks as a pure liability. But with a different perspective, I recognized this as a driver of efficiency and innovation. Because routine tasks were painful for my ADHD brain, I became adept at finding ways to streamline or automate them, often improving processes for everyone in the process.

The mindset shift didn't make the challenges of ADHD disappear. I still struggled with time management, still had to work to maintain focus on less engaging tasks, and still battled with organization and memory. But I stopped seeing these challenges as character flaws and started seeing them as specific hurdles to overcome with targeted strategies. And most importantly, I began to recognize and leverage the flip side of these challenges: the energy, creativity, and different perspective that came with my ADHD brain.

Self-Assessment: Identifying Your Unique ADHD Traits

Here's something crucial to understand: No two people with ADHD are exactly alike. The label encompasses a wide spectrum of traits that show up differently in each person. Some people are primarily inattentive, some are primarily hyperactive/impulsive, and many have a combined presentation with elements of both. Even within these categories, the specific manifestations vary widely.

Understanding your unique ADHD profile is essential for developing effective strategies. It's not enough to know you have ADHD; you need to know how your ADHD works.

For me, mapping my personal ADHD terrain was a process of discovery. I realized I had significant challenges with working memory, keeping information in mind while using it, which explained why I'd frequently lose my train of thought mid-sentence or forget what I was doing when I walked into a room. I discovered I had particular difficulty with time perception; I literally couldn't "feel" time passing in the way others seemed to, which explained my chronic lateness and tendency to hyperfocus for hours without realizing it.

On the other hand, I found I had strengths in creative problem-solving and pattern recognition. I could see connections between seemingly unrelated ideas and generate multiple possible solutions to problems. I also had good verbal skills and could be highly engaging when talking about topics that interested me.

This self-mapping became crucial for selecting and adapting strategies. Generic ADHD advice often failed me because it didn't address my specific profile.

Time has always had a strange way of slipping through my fingers. I'll start something thinking, "This will only take ten minutes," and before I know it, an hour has disappeared, gone without warning, like a magician's trick. Other times, it's the opposite. I plan an hour for something, finish it in ten minutes, and then those extra fifty minutes stretch endlessly, like waiting for a train that never comes. My sense of time has never really played by the same rules as everyone else's.

For instance, many ADHD resources recommend using digital calendars and reminder apps, and I've tried to control time with alarms and reminders, hoping structure could save me from the chaos. I'll set one for 1 p.m., thinking it will keep me accountable. However, when it rings, I hit snooze or reschedule it for later, around 2 p.m. or 3 p.m. It's not procrastination. It's that I'm usually buried in another task or simply not mentally ready to switch gears.

My brain needs time to transition, to warm up to the idea of what's next. Sometimes I keep snoozing until I finally have the mental space to tackle it. But if I hit "dismiss" before finishing, that's it, the reminder and the task are gone, swallowed by distraction.

Patience has never been my strong suit, which doesn't help. I want results now. I want to order now. But ADHD has a way of making time feel like quicksand. The harder I fight to control it, the deeper I sink.

I've tried visual reminders too: sticky notes, bright-colored stickers, motivational quotes taped to my desk. But after a few days, they fade into the background, swallowed by the noise of everyday life. What once screamed, "Don't forget me!" becomes just another part of the scenery. And in those moments, I can't help but laugh, because the tools meant to anchor me often get lost in the same storm they're supposed to calm.

To help you map your own ADHD terrain, consider these key areas:

- **Attention:** How does your attention work? Do you struggle more with focusing on tasks or with shifting attention between tasks? Can you hyperfocus on certain activities? Which activities capture your attention naturally, and which ones do you find almost impossible to engage with?

- **Executive function:** Which aspects of executive function are most challenging for you? Working memory? Planning and organization? Time management? Emotional regulation? Prioritization? Initiation (starting tasks)? Completion (finishing tasks)?

- **Energy regulation:** How does your energy fluctuate? Do you experience hyperactivity (physical or mental)? Sluggishness or fatigue? Does it vary by time of day or by type of task?

- **Sensory processing:** Are you more sensitive to sensory input than others? Do certain sounds, lights, textures, or other sensations particularly bother or distract you? Do you seek out sensory stimulation?

- **Emotional experience:** Do you experience emotions more intensely than others? Do you have difficulty regulating emotional responses? Do you experience rejection sensitivity?

- **Social interaction:** How does ADHD affect your social interactions? Do you interrupt others? Miss social cues? Hyperfocus on relationships? Struggle with reciprocity in conversations?

For each of these areas, also consider your strengths. Maybe your distractibility goes hand in hand with noticing details others miss. Maybe your impulsivity comes with spontaneity and quick decision-making in crises. Maybe your difficulty with routine tasks is balanced by creativity and innovative thinking.

In my case, I discovered that I worked best in environments with moderate background stimulation, enough to occupy the restless part of my brain but not so much that it overwhelmed me. Complete silence made my mind race with internal distractions, while too much unpredictable noise made it impossible to concentrate. This self-knowledge led me to seek out coffee shops with ambient noise for studying and to use instrumental music while working.

I also realized I had particular difficulty with task initiation, starting tasks, especially complex or boring ones. Once I understood this specific challenge, I could develop targeted strategies like breaking tasks into tiny first steps or using body-doubling (working alongside someone else) to overcome the initiation hurdle.

Understanding your unique ADHD profile isn't just about identifying challenges; it's about recognizing patterns and developing self-awareness that forms the foundation for everything else. It's about knowing when your ADHD traits might cause problems and when they might actually give you an edge.

This reframing, from seeing ADHD as a disorder to recognizing it as a different brain wiring with both challenges and strengths, changes everything. It doesn't eliminate the difficulties, but it puts them in a new light. It opens the door to strategies based not on becoming someone you're not, but on becoming the best version of who you actually are.

Key Takeaways

- **ADHD isn't a character flaw:** It's different brain wiring. Your challenges with focus, time, and impulse control stem from neurological differences in dopamine processing and brain structure, not laziness or lack of discipline.

- **Your ADHD brain has real strengths:** Creativity, hyperfocus, divergent thinking, resilience, and heightened empathy are directly connected to the same traits that create challenges, and they're valuable.

- **Mindset is the foundation:** How you think about your ADHD shapes everything else. A growth mindset that sees ADHD as different (not broken) opens the door to working with your brain instead of against it.

- **Reframe the narrative:** Stop asking "What's wrong with me?" and start asking "How does my brain work? How can I work with it?" This shift from shame to curiosity changes everything.

- **Your unique ADHD profile matters:** Everyone with ADHD experiences it differently. Understanding your specific challenges and strengths—not generic ADHD traits—is the foundation for developing strategies that actually work for you.

In the next chapter, we'll build on this foundation by exploring specific techniques for finding focus when your attention naturally wanders. We'll look at how to create environments that support your ADHD brain rather than fight against it and how to leverage the natural tendencies of your mind to achieve the focus you need when you need it.

CHAPTER 2

HARNESS YOUR ATTENTION

FINDING FOCUS IN THE FRENZY

———◆◇◆———

"Focus harder."

That's what they tell us, isn't it? Like we haven't been trying that our entire lives. Like we just never thought of it before.

I remember sitting at my kitchen table, surrounded by CPA exam materials, feeling like I was underwater. The words on the page kept swimming before my eyes. I'd read a paragraph, get to the end, and realize I hadn't absorbed a single word. So I'd read it again. And again. Sometimes I'd read the same paragraph five times and still have no idea what it said.

Meanwhile, my brain was busy noticing everything else. The faint hum of the refrigerator. The neighbor's dog barking two houses down. The way the afternoon light hit the wall in a particular pattern. The sudden urgent question of whether penguins have knees. The memory of an embarrassing thing I said at a party three years ago.

Everything except the material I desperately needed to learn.

It was maddening. The more I tried to force my focus, the more my mind rebelled. The harder I pushed, the more scattered I became. And the whole time, a voice in my head kept saying, "What's wrong with you? Why can't you just concentrate like a normal person?"

I'm guessing you know exactly what I'm talking about. That feeling of your attention constantly slipping through your fingers like water, no matter how tightly you try to grasp it. The frustration of knowing you're smart enough to understand the material, but somehow can't make your brain cooperate. The shame of watching others seemingly focus effortlessly while you struggle to stay on task for even fifteen minutes.

This chapter builds the "H" pillar of the *THRIVE ADHD Success Formula*. While Chapter 1 reframed how you think about ADHD, this chapter gives you concrete tools for managing attention in a brain that struggles with focus on demand. You'll learn that ADHD isn't about lacking attention; it's about difficulty directing attention. The strategies here are about creating conditions that help your brain engage naturally.

Understanding the ADHD Attention System

Focused Attention | Hyperfocus | Scattered | Background Attention

In a neurotypical brain, there's a pretty smooth handoff between different attention networks. When someone needs to focus on a task, their brain efficiently quiets down the "default mode network," the part responsible for daydreaming, self-reflection, and mind-wandering, and ramps up the "executive function network," the part that handles focused attention, working memory, and goal-directed behavior.

But in the ADHD brain, this handoff is bumpy. The default mode network doesn't quiet down properly when we need to focus. It keeps chattering away in the background, serving up random thoughts, memories, worries, and ideas while we're trying to concentrate on something specific. Meanwhile, our executive function network, which should be running the show during focused tasks, keeps flickering like a light bulb with a loose connection.

This isn't because we're not trying hard enough. It's literally how our brains are wired. And it explains so much about the ADHD experience.

It explains why we can read the same paragraph five times without absorbing it, then suddenly realize we've been thinking about something completely unrelated the whole time. It explains why we might completely lose track of time when doing something engaging (hyperfocus) but feel every excruciating second when doing something boring. It explains why traditional advice like "just eliminate all distractions" often backfires for us.

I experienced this constantly during my graduate coursework. I remember sitting in a three-hour evening accounting class after a full day of work, desperately trying to follow the professor's explanation of complex tax regulations. I'd start off strong, taking notes and following along. Then, without warning, my mind would drift. By the time I caught myself, the professor had moved on to an entirely different topic, and I'd missed crucial information.

Or when I was studying for the CPA exam's Financial Accounting and Reporting section, I'd sit down with my textbook, determined to get through a chapter. Two hours later, I'd realized I'd read only three pages because I kept spacing out mid-paragraph. Each time I caught myself drifting, I'd go back to where I lost focus, only to drift again moments later. The cycle was exhausting and demoralizing.

What made it worse was the anxiety that built up around this struggle. As deadlines loomed, my stress increased. And ironically, the more stressed I became about my inability to focus, the harder focusing became. It was a vicious cycle that led to many late nights of panic-driven cramming and a persistent feeling that I just wasn't cut out for this level of academic work.

What I didn't understand then, but know now, is that my attention system wasn't broken; it was just different. The ADHD brain is constantly seeking the optimal level of stimulation. When a task doesn't provide enough stimulation (like reading a dry accounting textbook), our brain starts looking elsewhere for it. This isn't a moral failing or lack of discipline; it's our brain's natural response to understimulation.

Understanding this was the first step toward finding solutions. If my brain needed a certain level of stimulation to function optimally, then the key wasn't eliminating all stimulation (the traditional advice). It was finding the right kind and amount of stimulation to keep my brain engaged without overwhelming it.

This realization completely changed my approach to studying and working. Instead of fighting against my brain's need for stimulation, I started working with it. And that made all the difference.

Creating Focus-Supporting Environments

An ADHD-friendly attention toolkit

Your physical environment has a huge impact on your ability to focus, especially with ADHD. What works for neurotypical people often doesn't work for us.

The standard advice is to eliminate all distractions. Study in a quiet library. Clear your desk of everything except what you're working on. Turn off all music and sounds. For some people, this creates the perfect focus environment. For many with ADHD, it's torture.

In complete silence, with nothing to occupy the stimulus-seeking part of our brains, our internal distractions often become louder and more insistent. That's when you start counting ceiling tiles, contemplating the meaning of life, or suddenly remembering every embarrassing thing you've ever done.

I discovered this the hard way. When I started studying for the CPA exam, I followed all the traditional advice. I found the quietest corner of the university library. I cleared my desk of everything except my textbook and notebook. I turned off my phone. And I was absolutely miserable. My mind raced from thought to thought. The silence felt oppressive. I'd leave after an hour, having accomplished almost nothing, convinced there was something deeply wrong with me.

Then one day, out of desperation, I tried something different. Instead of the silent library, I went to a coffee shop. Instead of sitting perfectly still, I brought a small fidget toy to keep my hands busy. Instead of silence, I put on instrumental music through my headphones. And something amazing happened; I actually got work done. Not perfectly, not without any distractions, but significantly better than in my "distraction-free" environment.

This was a revelation. My optimal study environment wasn't the same as what worked for others. Through trial and error, I gradually figured out what conditions helped my particular ADHD brain function best:

- **Background noise:** Not silence, not chaotic noise, but a steady ambient hum (coffee shop noise, rainfall sounds, or instrumental music).

- **Visual environment:** Not completely stark, but not cluttered with interesting things either. A balance where my eyes could rest somewhere neutral when needed.

- **Lighting:** Natural light when possible, but not sitting directly facing a window where I'd be distracted by everything happening outside.

- **Temperature:** Slightly cool rather than warm. Warmth made me sleepy and even less focused.

- **Seating:** Comfortable enough that I wasn't distracted by discomfort, but not so comfortable that I'd drift off or lose alertness.

- **Movement options:** The freedom to fidget, shift positions, or occasionally get up and stretch without disrupting others.

Your ideal environment might be completely different from mine; that's the thing about ADHD: It affects each of us uniquely. The key is to experiment systematically rather than assuming what works for others will work for you.

Try studying in different locations with varying levels of background noise. Notice when you're most productive. Pay attention to how the time of day affects your focus. Keep track of what elements seem to help and which ones hinder. It's not about finding the perfect environment (which doesn't exist) but about creating conditions that work *with* your brain instead of against it.

Strategic Use of Background Stimulation

This might sound counterintuitive, but one of the most effective focus tools in my ADHD tool kit is strategic background stimulation. Not random distractions, but carefully chosen background input that actually *helps* maintain focus rather than breaking it.

Here's the theory behind why this works: The ADHD brain is constantly seeking an optimal level of stimulation. When a task doesn't provide enough stimulation (like reading a textbook), our brain starts looking elsewhere for it: internal thoughts, environmental distractions, anything to reach that optimal stimulation level.

By intentionally providing some background stimulation, you can satisfy that seeking part of your brain so it doesn't go hunting for more disruptive distractions. It's like giving your hyperactive puppy a chew toy so it doesn't destroy your furniture.

My personal breakthrough came one night when I was desperate to get through some particularly dry material on corporate tax regulations. Out of frustration, I put on an episode of *Friends* in the background, a show I'd seen so many times I could practically recite the dialogue. To my surprise, I found myself able to read and comprehend the material much better than in silence.

Why did this work? The familiar show provided just enough background stimulation to occupy the restless part of my brain without being engaging enough to capture my full attention. It was the perfect level of distraction; just enough to prevent my mind from seeking more disruptive distractions.

I refined this technique over time. For highly complex material requiring deep thought, I'd use instrumental music or ambient sounds (rainfall, coffee shop noise) through headphones. For moderately difficult material or practice problems, familiar TV shows playing softly in the background worked well. For rote memorization tasks, more engaging background noise sometimes helped maintain motivation.

The key is finding the right match between task complexity and background stimulation. More complex tasks generally need less or simpler background stimulation. Simpler, more repetitive tasks might benefit from slightly more engaging background input to maintain interest.

Some options to experiment with include:

- **Instrumental music:** Film scores work well because they're designed to enhance rather than distract from what's happening on screen. Classical, lo-fi, ambient electronic, or jazz can also work depending on your taste.

- **Nature sounds:** Rainfall, ocean waves, forest sounds, anything steady and non-jarring.

- **Coffee shop noise:** There are actually apps and websites that recreate the ambient hum of cafés.

- **Familiar TV shows:** The key is familiarity, like shows you've seen multiple times, so they don't pull your attention away with new plot developments.

- **White noise or fan sounds:** Simple, consistent background noise that masks other environmental sounds.

This isn't just my personal quirk. Research supports that some people with ADHD actually focus better with moderate background noise (Söderlund et al., 2007).

The right background stimulation varies from person to person and task to task. What works for me might not work for you. The key is experimenting mindfully, paying attention to what conditions help you focus best on different types of tasks.

Body-Doubling and Accountability Systems

Have you ever noticed you can focus better when someone else is working nearby? Maybe you're more productive in a coffee shop full of other people working than alone in your quiet home office. Or perhaps you find it easier to tackle household chores when a friend comes over to help, even if they're working on something entirely different.

This phenomenon is called "body-doubling," and it's a powerful tool for many people with ADHD.

Body-doubling simply means having another person present (physically or virtually) while you work on tasks that require focus. The other person doesn't need to help with your work or even understand it; their presence alone can help anchor your attention and regulate your focus.

Why Body-Doubling Works

Why does this work? Several reasons, which are:

- **External accountability:** Knowing someone else can see whether you're working or distracted adds gentle pressure to stay on task.

- **Reduced working memory load:** Having someone else present can help keep you aware of time passing and maintain awareness of your goals without having to actively remember them yourself.

- **Mirror neurons:** Our brains are naturally wired to sync up with others nearby, so being around focused people can help us focus, too.

- **Reduced isolation:** ADHD tasks can feel lonely and overwhelming, and having company makes them more manageable emotionally.

I discovered the power of body-doubling during my master's program when I joined a study group for my advanced accounting course. Even though we each worked on our own assignments, something about having others around who were also focused and working toward similar goals helped me maintain concentration for much longer periods.

Later, when studying for the CPA exam, I'd arrange to meet a friend at a coffee shop. We'd work on completely different things—me on exam prep, her on her own projects—but the accountability of having someone there kept me from falling into distractions or giving up when the material got challenging.

How to Implement Body-Doubling

You can implement body-doubling in many ways:

- in-person study or work sessions with friends, classmates, or colleagues

- virtual co-working sessions using video calls, where everyone works silently on their own tasks

- accountability partnerships where you check in with each other regularly

- formal or informal study groups

- working in public spaces like libraries or coffee shops

- using co-working apps that connect you with random

people for focus sessions

The key is finding the right balance; someone whose presence helps you focus rather than becoming a distraction themselves. Some people work better with a friend nearby, while others do better with strangers (less temptation to chat). Some prefer in-person body-doubling, while others find virtual works just as well.

During my CPA exam preparation, I found that different types of body-doubling worked for different tasks. For initial learning of new material, I preferred studying alone. For practice problems and review, having a study buddy helped me stay motivated and push through difficult sections. For the final review before the exam, studying in a library where others were also intensely focused created the perfect environment for sustained concentration.

Breaking Tasks Into ADHD-Friendly Segments

One of the quickest ways to paralyze the ADHD brain is to present it with a massive, undefined task. "Study for the exam." "Write the report." "Clean the house." These vague, overwhelming directives are kryptonite to our executive function.

The ADHD brain often struggles with what's called "task initiation," or starting tasks, especially ones that seem large or complex. We look at the mountain we need to climb and get stuck in a loop of overwhelm, procrastination, and anxiety. Even when we do start, sustaining attention for the duration of a large project can feel impossible.

The solution? Break everything down into ridiculously small pieces.

This was a game-changer for me during CPA exam preparation. Instead of telling myself, "I need to study audit today," a vague goal that immediately overwhelmed me, I'd break it into tiny, concrete steps:

- "I'm going to read pages 42-45."

- "I'm going to do 10 practice questions on inventory valuation."

- "I'm going to watch one video lecture on sampling methods."

These tiny goals gave me clear starting points, clear endpoints, and a sense of accomplishment as I completed each one. Instead of feeling like I was making no progress on an endless task, I could see myself completing specific segments.

For the Regulation section of the CPA exam, which covers tax law and business law, I created what I called "micro-modules." Each covered a super-specific topic, like "S Corporation Distributions" or "Contract Breach Remedies," and included just two to three pages of reading, 5-10 practice questions, and maybe a short video. I could complete one micro-module in about 20-30 minutes, which matched my natural attention span much better than trying to study "tax law" for three hours.

How to Break Down Tasks

There are several techniques you can use for breaking down tasks:

- **The "Swiss cheese" method:** Instead of tackling a project from beginning to end, poke "holes" in it by completing small parts that appeal to you. Eventually, these holes connect, and the whole project becomes more manageable.

- **Task slicing:** Cut work into 5-15 minute segments. Don't think about the whole project, just the current slice.

- **Mini-milestones:** Create frequent achievement points where you can pause, assess progress, and give yourself credit for what you've completed.

- **The "next physical action" approach:** Instead of writing down vague goals like "work on the project," identify the exact next physical action: "Open the Word document and write the first paragraph of the introduction," or "Call Jim to ask about quarterly sales figures."

For my Financial Accounting and Reporting exam preparation, which covered the most material of all four CPA exam sections, I created a system where each study session began with me identifying three tiny goals. Not "review pension accounting," but "do practice questions 1-5 on pension expense calculation," "reread the example on page 237," and "watch the 10-minute video explanation on corridor amortization."

This approach works for several reasons. First, it reduces the activation energy needed to start. Beginning a 10-minute task is far less daunting than beginning an amorphous multi-hour project. Second, it provides frequent dopamine hits as you complete each small segment, which the ADHD brain desperately needs for motivation. Third, it makes progress visible and concrete, countering the common ADHD experience of feeling like you're working hard but getting nowhere.

There's no task too small to break down further. If even your small tasks feel overwhelming, break them into even smaller pieces. What matters isn't how impressive each step looks, but that you're moving forward consistently.

Practical Tools: Timers, Apps, and Physical Aids

Sometimes the simplest tools make the biggest difference for ADHD focus. Let's talk about some concrete aids that can help externalize your attention system and make focus more manageable.

Timers were absolutely crucial during my CPA exam preparation. Not just any timers, but specifically visual timers that showed time passing in a concrete way. The *Time Timer* became my best friend; a device with a red disk that gradually disappears as time passes, making time visible in a way that the ADHD brain can process.

I used timers in several ways. The most effective was a modified Pomodoro Technique, working in focused intervals with breaks in between. Traditional Pomodoro suggests 25 minutes of work followed by 5 minutes of break, but I found that wasn't optimal for my ADHD brain. Through experimentation, I discovered my personal sweet spot was about 32 minutes of focus followed by 8 minutes of break. This was just enough time to get into a flow state, but not so long that my focus completely crashed.

The key modification for ADHD is flexibility with the intervals. On good focus days, I might stretch to 40-45-minute work periods.

On tough days, even 15 minutes of solid focus was a win. The point isn't to force yourself into a rigid system but to work with your brain's natural rhythms while providing just enough external structure to support sustained attention.

During breaks, I'd do something completely different: stretch, get water, look out the window, or do a quick household task. The physical movement and change of focus gave my brain the novelty and stimulation it craved, making it easier to return to focused work afterward.

Beyond timers, I found several other tools invaluable:

- **Noise-canceling headphones:** These were essential for studying in public places or when my roommates were home. They didn't just block distracting sounds but created a sort of "focus bubble" that helped signal to my brain that it was time to concentrate.

- **Fidget tools:** Having something to do with my hands made it much easier to keep my body still and my mind engaged. I rotated between a stress ball, a fidget cube, and even just a paperclip to bend during study sessions.

- **External working memory aids:** Sticky notes, whiteboards, and digital task managers offloaded the working memory demands that often overwhelm the ADHD brain. Instead of trying to hold information in my head (where it would invariably slip away), I externalized it.

- **Visual blockers:** For reading dense text, I used a simple index card to cover lines I wasn't currently reading. This prevented my eyes (and attention) from constantly jumping ahead or around the page.

- **Text-to-speech software:** For particularly dry or difficult material, having it read aloud while I followed along engaged an additional sensory channel and helped maintain focus.

- **Ambient focus apps:** Programs like Focus@Will that provide background sounds specifically designed to enhance concentration.

The key with all these tools is personalization and experimentation. What works for one person with ADHD might be useless or even counterproductive for another. The goal is to build your own personal tool kit of resources you can deploy depending on the specific focus challenges you're facing that day.

Doodling and Fidgeting for Focus

"Stop fidgeting and pay attention!"

If you grew up with ADHD, you probably heard some version of this more times than you can count. It's rooted in the assumption that physical stillness equals mental focus; an assumption that's actually backward for many ADHD brains.

One of my biggest breakthroughs came when I realized that movement, specifically controlled fidgeting and doodling, actually helped my focus rather than hindered it.

During long accounting lectures, I'd fill the margins of my notes with abstract patterns, geometric shapes, and random doodles.

I wasn't doing this because I was bored or not paying attention. I was doing it because it helped me pay attention. The simple, repetitive hand movements seemed to occupy just enough of my brain to prevent it from completely wandering off while still allowing me to process what the professor was saying.

Similarly, when reading textbooks or studying for long periods, I found that having something to fidget with—a stress ball, a fidget cube, or even a paperclip to bend—helped me maintain focus much better than trying to sit completely still. The small physical movements provided just enough sensory input to satisfy my brain's need for stimulation without becoming a full-blown distraction.

There's actually solid science behind this. Research suggests that for many people with ADHD, certain types of physical movement can help regulate attention by (Martín-Rodríguez et al., 2025):

- increasing arousal in underactive brain regions needed for focus.

- providing sensory input that helps filter out other distractions.

- occupying the brain's need for stimulation so it doesn't seek it elsewhere.

- burning off excess energy that might otherwise manifest as mental restlessness.

The key is finding the right kind and amount of movement. Not all fidgeting is created equal. Some types are more helpful than others, and what works in one situation might be too distracting in another.

Helpful fidgeting tends to be:

- repetitive and doesn't require much thought.

- relatively quiet and unobtrusive.

- something you can do without looking at it.

- not so interesting that it becomes the focus itself.

For doodling, I found that abstract patterns worked better than attempting to draw actual objects or scenes. The former occupied just enough attention to be helpful, while the latter could become too engaging and pull me away from what I was supposed to be focusing on.

During my CPA exam studies, I developed a whole arsenal of focus-supporting movements. Those included:

- squeezing a stress ball while reading

- tapping a pencil eraser silently against my leg during lectures

- doodling geometric patterns while listening to audio material

- using a fidget cube under my desk during study groups

- gentle rocking or swaying while working on practice problems

These movements weren't distractions; they were concentration aids. They helped channel excess energy and satisfy my brain's need for stimulation in a controlled way that actually supported sustained attention.

If you've been fighting against your natural tendency to move while focusing, try embracing it instead. Experiment with different types of fidgeting and doodling to find what helps your particular brain. Just make sure your movement choices don't create new distractions for yourself or others.

Managing Digital Distractions

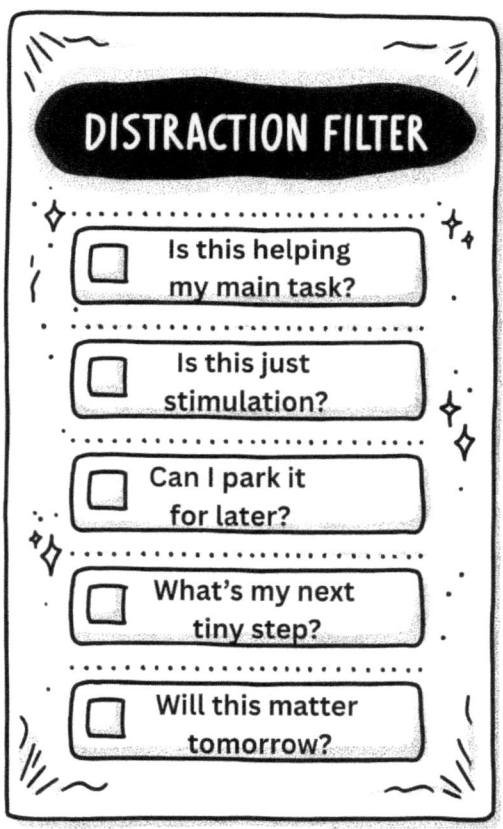

Digital technology is both a blessing and a curse for the ADHD brain. On one hand, it gives us incredible tools for organization, learning, and productivity. On the other hand, it's an unprecedented distraction machine perfectly engineered to capture and fragment our already vulnerable attention.

During my CPA exam preparation, I had to confront my relationship with digital distraction head-on. I was studying in the evenings after work, already mentally tired, and the siren song of social media, news sites, and random internet rabbit holes was nearly impossible to resist. I'd sit down to study, and somehow 45 minutes would vanish into the digital ether with nothing accomplished.

What made digital distractions especially dangerous was how quickly and seamlessly they could capture my attention. Checking a single notification could lead to 30 minutes of mindless scrolling before I even realized what was happening. And each of these attention shifts made it harder to get back on task.

Through painful trial and error, I developed a system for managing digital distractions that worked with my ADHD brain rather than against it. Here's what helped.

First, I had to acknowledge that complete digital abstinence wasn't realistic or necessary. The goal wasn't to eliminate all digital interaction but to gain control over when and how I engaged with it.

I started using website blockers during study sessions. Apps like *Freedom*, *Cold Turkey*, and *StayFocusd* allowed me to temporarily block distracting websites and apps. The key was that they created a small barrier between impulse and action, just enough friction to give my prefrontal cortex a chance to catch up with my impulses.

I also discovered the power of scheduled distraction. Instead of trying to ignore the pull of social media or news (which paradoxically made it stronger), I built short, defined periods for checking these sites into my study schedule. "After I complete these 20 practice questions, I can check Instagram for 5 minutes." This worked far better than trying to resist indefinitely because it gave my brain something to look forward to and satisfied my need for digital stimulation in a controlled way.

Another effective approach was creating separate digital environments for different purposes. On my laptop, I set up different user profiles: one for studying with minimal apps and websites available, and one for personal use with everything accessible. This created a clear boundary between work mode and play mode.

For my phone, I used a similar approach with focus modes that limited which apps could send notifications during study times. I also removed social media apps from my home screen, requiring an extra step to access them and giving me a moment to reconsider before diving in.

Perhaps most important was rearranging my digital environment to remove cues that triggered distracting habits. I logged out of social media accounts so I'd have to consciously log in rather than checking them automatically. I turned off almost all notifications. I installed browser extensions that replaced distracting elements on websites with motivational messages or blank spaces.

The digital strategies that worked best weren't about pure willpower; they were about thoughtfully engineering my environment to support my goals rather than undermine them. They acknowledged my brain's natural tendencies and chose to work *with* them rather than against them.

By the time I was preparing for my final CPA exam section, I had developed such effective digital management habits that technology had transformed from my biggest distraction into one of my most powerful study tools. I could use online practice questions, video lectures, and digital flashcards without constantly falling into distraction traps.

Building an effective ADHD attention tool kit isn't about becoming someone you're not. It's about understanding your unique brain and creating conditions that help it function at its best.

No single technique will work perfectly all the time. The key is having multiple strategies you can deploy depending on the day, the task, and your current mental state. Some days you'll need more structure, other days more flexibility. Some tasks will require one approach, other tasks something completely different.

Key Takeaways

- **ADHD attention isn't broken:** It's differently regulated. Your brain struggles to quiet the default mode network and engage executive function on demand, especially for unstimulating tasks. This is neurology, not laziness.

- **Your environment is your attention system:** Strategic background stimulation, proper lighting, comfortable seating, and sensory-friendly spaces can dramatically improve focus. Create an environment that works for your brain, not against it.

- **Break tasks into ridiculously small pieces:** Large, vague projects trigger overwhelm and procrastination. Micro-modules with clear endpoints and frequent rewards align with how the ADHD brain sustains motivation and attention.

- **Use external tools to support focus:** Timers, fidget tools, body-doubling, doodling, and strategic use of background noise are regulation tools that help your brain stay engaged.

- **Digital distractions require digital solutions:** Website blockers, scheduled distraction time, and careful notification management create friction between impulse and action, giving your prefrontal cortex time to catch up.

In the next chapter, we'll tackle another major ADHD challenge: managing time when your brain doesn't perceive it the same way others do. We'll explore strategies for navigating deadlines, scheduling, and time estimation when you're "time blind," and how to leverage your ADHD brain's unique relationship with time to your advantage.

CHAPTER 3

REGULATE YOUR TIME

MASTERING TIME WHEN YOU'RE "TIME BLIND"

───────◆○◆───────

Have you ever looked at the clock, certain only fifteen minutes had passed, only to discover it's been two hours? Or had the opposite experience, a twenty-minute task somehow consuming your entire afternoon?

I remember sitting down "just to check one email" before starting my CPA exam prep one evening. The next time I looked up, somehow three hours had vanished. It was now 11 p.m., I hadn't studied at all, and I couldn't even tell you what I'd been doing online for those lost hours. The panic and self-loathing that followed were all too familiar: why couldn't I just manage my time like a normal adult?

Another day, I'd promised myself I'd start studying by 9 a.m. But first, I needed coffee. And while waiting for the coffee, I noticed the kitchen counter needed wiping. Which made me realize the trash needed to be taken out. Which reminded me I'd meant to text my friend back yesterday. Suddenly, it was noon, my study materials remained untouched, and I felt like a complete failure before I'd even begun.

Sound familiar? If so, you're experiencing what many ADHD experts call time blindness: a genuine difference in how your brain perceives and processes time.

This chapter builds the "R" pillar of the *THRIVE ADHD Success Formula*. Time blindness is one of the most frustrating aspects of ADHD. Your brain simply doesn't perceive time the way neurotypical brains do. Rather than fighting this neurological reality, this pillar is about making time external and visible. You'll learn to build systems that compensate for your unreliable internal clock, break the procrastination-crisis cycle, and transform your relationship with deadlines and schedules.

Understanding ADHD Time Perception Differences

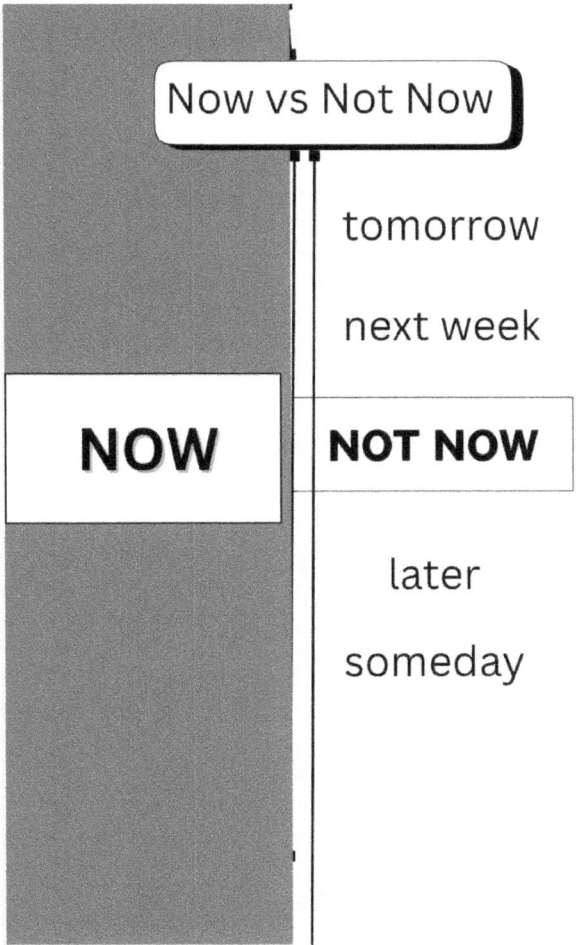

The ADHD brain experiences time differently than the neurotypical brain. Neurotypical brains have a fairly accurate internal clock. They can sense roughly how much time has passed without looking at a clock. They can reliably estimate how long a task will take. And perhaps most importantly, they can feel the future approaching; tomorrow's deadline creates a sense of urgency today.

But the ADHD brain has what some researchers call temporal myopia: a nearsightedness when it comes to time. The future feels abstract and distant until suddenly it's crashing down on you. There are often just two time zones: Now and Not Now. Anything that's not happening right this minute, whether it's due tomorrow or in three months, can feel equally distant and unreal.

I experienced this constantly while preparing for the CPA exam. Despite having a study schedule mapped out months in advance, each evening I'd sit down to study as if the exam date were some abstract concept rather than a concrete reality steadily approaching. I couldn't feel the pressure of time passing until I was down to the final days, when suddenly panic would set in.

This time perception difference affected me in countless ways.

I chronically underestimated how long tasks would take. What I thought would be a quick thirty-minute review of a chapter would consistently take two hours or more.

I struggled to connect present actions with future consequences. Even though logically I knew that studying today would help me pass the exam later, emotionally it felt like future-me was a different person entirely.

Time seemed to move at wildly different speeds depending on what I was doing. When I was engaged in something interesting (even if unrelated to my goals), hours would vanish in what felt like minutes. But when forcing myself through a difficult study session, every minute crawled by with excruciating slowness.

I lived in a constant cycle of procrastination followed by crisis. I'd put off starting assignments until the deadline loomed so large it finally felt real, then pull all-nighters to finish just in time, exhausting myself in the process.

One particularly vivid example is: For a graduate-level tax accounting course, I had an entire semester to complete a complex research project. Despite setting calendar reminders and scheduling study sessions, I couldn't make myself start early. The deadline remained abstract until exactly three days before it was due, when suddenly the future became present, and I went into crisis mode. I barely slept for 72 hours, completed the project, and earned a good grade, but at a tremendous personal cost of stress, exhaustion, and self-recrimination.

What I didn't understand then was that this wasn't a moral failing. My brain literally couldn't feel the urgency of a deadline until it was imminent. My time perception was fundamentally different from what was expected in academic and professional settings.

When you recognize that your challenges with time aren't due to laziness or lack of care but to genuine neurological differences, you can stop beating yourself up and start building systems that compensate for these differences.

External Time Management Systems

When your internal clock is unreliable, the solution is to make time external and visible. Think of it like this: If you were physically blind, you wouldn't try to navigate by forcing yourself to see; you'd use tools like a cane, Braille, or audio cues to compensate. Similarly, if you're "time blind," you need external tools to make time concrete and visible.

During my CPA exam preparation, I gradually built an external time management system that compensated for my unreliable internal clock. I didn't realize it then, but I was creating what ADHD experts now call prosthetic time management: external tools that serve the time-tracking function my brain struggled with.

The centerpiece of my system was a large wall calendar that hung directly above my desk. Not a digital calendar hidden in my phone or computer, but a physical calendar where I could see entire months at once. I marked exam dates in red, assignment deadlines in blue, and self-imposed milestones in green. This gave time a visual dimension; I could literally see time passing and deadlines approaching.

Next to this calendar, I kept a whiteboard with my weekly to-do list. Again, the key was visibility, not a list hidden in a planner or app, but something I couldn't avoid seeing multiple times per day. I broke big projects down into concrete next actions and used different colors for different subjects or priority levels.

I also became religious about using timers and alarms. I discovered that while I couldn't reliably sense how much time had passed, I could respond to external time cues. I used a kitchen timer (the old-school kind where you can see the time ticking down) for study sessions. I'd set it for 30 minutes, and seeing the time visibly decreasing helped anchor me in reality.

For transitions between activities, I'd set alarms on my phone with specific labels: "Wrap up email and start studying" or "Begin review of chapter 3." I needed these external prompts because internal transitions, deciding on my own to stop one activity and start another, were extremely difficult.

Another crucial tool was my time block planner. Unlike traditional planners that just list appointments, this one divided each day into concrete blocks of time. I'd literally color in the blocks I planned to use for studying, creating a visual representation of how I intended to use my time each day. Did I always stick perfectly to this schedule? Absolutely not. But it made time concrete in a way my brain could process.

For deadlines and important events, I used a countdown app on my phone that showed exactly how many days remained until my exam date. This helped make the future more concrete by translating it into a steadily decreasing number I could see every day.

These external systems weren't perfect. There were still days when I lost track of time or procrastinated until the last minute. But they significantly reduced the frequency and severity of time-related crises. More importantly, they reduced the emotional toll of constantly feeling like I was failing at basic adult time management.

How to Build an External Time Management System

If you're building your own external time management system, experiment with the tools below to find what works for your specific brain:

- visual timers where you can see time passing (*Time Timer* is a popular brand designed specifically for this purpose)

- wall calendars or large desk calendars that make time visible at a glance

- physical to-do lists positioned where you'll see them multiple times daily

- alarms labeled with specific transition prompts ("Stop scrolling and start working")

- apps that visualize time passing or count down to important dates

- time-blocking planners that represent time as physical space to be filled

The key is making time tangible, visible, and unavoidable rather than abstract and easy to ignore. Your external system should compensate for exactly what your particular brain struggles with most.

Breaking the Procrastination-Crisis Cycle

One of the most painful patterns with ADHD time blindness is the procrastination-crisis cycle. You know you should start a task well before the deadline. You fully intend to start early. But somehow you can't make yourself begin until panic sets in at the last minute, triggering a frantic rush to finish just in time.

This cycle is exhausting, stressful, and reinforces negative beliefs about yourself. But it happens for neurological reasons, not moral ones. The ADHD brain often requires higher levels of interest, novelty, challenge, or urgency to engage the neural networks needed for focused work. A far-off deadline simply doesn't create enough activation for many ADHD brains to overcome the initial hurdle of starting.

I lived in this cycle for years, especially during my accounting studies. For one advanced financial accounting class, I had a major case study due at the end of the semester. Despite my best intentions and a detailed schedule for working on it gradually, I couldn't make myself start until just three days before it was due. The project required analyzing complex financial statements, preparing adjusting entries, and writing explanations for numerous accounting treatments. It was easily 20+ hours of work that I compressed into three sleepless days and nights of frantic activity.

I earned a good grade, but the physical and emotional cost was tremendous: exhaustion, self-loathing, and reinforcement of the belief that I could only work under extreme pressure. This pattern continued through much of my education and early career until I finally developed strategies to break the cycle.

The key breakthrough came when I realized I needed to artificially create the conditions that helped my brain activate, rather than waiting for them to occur naturally as deadlines approached. I needed to manufacture urgency, interest, and novelty earlier in the process.

Artificial Deadlines

One of the most effective techniques was creating artificial deadlines well before the real ones. For my final CPA exam section, I set a "personal deadline" exactly two weeks before the actual exam date. I told friends and family this was my real deadline. I scheduled a small celebration for meeting this deadline. I even created tangible consequences for missing it (if I wasn't fully prepared by my artificial deadline, I'd have to donate to a cause I didn't support).

This wasn't just wishful thinking; I built concrete structures around these self-imposed deadlines to make them feel real. I'd schedule a practice exam for my artificial deadline date. I'd arrange to meet with a study buddy to review material. I'd book a restaurant for a small celebration dinner. These external commitments helped create the sense of urgency my brain needed to activate.

Task Appetizers

Another technique was what I call task appetizers: making the start of a task so absurdly small and easy that it bypassed my brain's resistance to beginning. Instead of "Study chapter 4," my to-do list might say, "Open textbook to chapter 4 and read just the first paragraph." The act of starting was usually the biggest hurdle; once I'd read that first paragraph, continuing was much easier.

Social Accountability

I also learned to leverage social accountability. I'd tell a friend I was going to complete a specific study task by a certain time, then check in with them afterward. Sometimes I'd even use body-doubling, which mysteriously makes initiating and sustaining work easier for many ADHD brains.

Self-Compassion

Perhaps most important was developing self-compassion around this pattern. When I stopped viewing my procrastination as a moral failing and started seeing it as a neurological difference I was actively working to accommodate, the shame spiral lessened. This reduced my anxiety, which actually made it easier to start tasks earlier.

The "Small Chunks + Rewards" System

One of the most powerful strategies I discovered for managing ADHD time challenges was what I call the "Small Chunks + Rewards" system. This approach works with your brain's dopamine system rather than fighting against it.

Here's the basic premise: The ADHD brain struggles with dopamine regulation, which affects motivation, reward processing, and the ability to delay gratification. Traditional approaches to large projects—work consistently for long periods, delay rewards until completion—are fundamentally mismatched to how the ADHD brain functions.

Instead, this system breaks tasks into tiny pieces and pairs each small accomplishment with an immediate reward. This provides the frequent dopamine hits the ADHD brain needs to sustain motivation and makes large projects manageable by transforming them into a series of small wins.

I developed this system during my CPA exam preparation almost by accident. Initially, I tried to force myself to study the way I thought I should: long, uninterrupted sessions working through practice tests or textbook chapters. This inevitably led to frustration, as my attention would wander long before I completed these marathon sessions.

After numerous failures, I tried a different approach. Instead of attempting to complete an entire 100-question practice test in one sitting, I broke it into sets of just 10 questions. After completing each set, I gave myself a small, immediate reward: five minutes of stretching, a quick snack, a few minutes watching a favorite TV show, or just stepping outside for fresh air.

The transformation was remarkable. Instead of dreading a four-hour study session, I looked forward to the series of small challenges and rewards. My brain could handle focusing on just 10 questions, knowing a break was coming soon. And the satisfaction of completing each small chunk created momentum that carried me through the entire project.

I applied this same system to reading dense textbook material. Rather than assigning myself an entire chapter, I'd break it into three- to five-page segments. After each segment, I'd take a very short break or give myself a small reward. This made seemingly insurmountable reading assignments approachable and doable.

For particularly challenging topics, I'd make the chunks even smaller, sometimes as little as reading a single page or working through just one complex problem. The key was matching the chunk size to my current attention capacity and the difficulty of the material.

The rewards were equally important. I discovered they didn't need to be elaborate or time-consuming, just something my brain registered as pleasant. Sometimes it was as simple as making a checkmark on my tracking sheet (the visual representation of progress is itself rewarding to many ADHD brains). Other times it might be a piece of chocolate, a quick social media check, or a few minutes of a favorite song.

What made this system so effective was that it worked with my brain's natural functioning. Traditional approaches assume you can sustain motivation through sheer willpower until a distant reward. This system acknowledges that the ADHD brain needs more frequent dopamine hits to maintain engagement and provides them in a structured, intentional way.

How to Implement Small Chunks + Rewards System

To implement your own Small Chunks + Rewards system:

1. Analyze your typical attention span for different types of tasks (it may be shorter than you think).

2. Break projects into chunks that fit within or slightly below that attention span.

3. Identify small, immediate rewards that you genuinely enjoy.

4. Create a visual tracking system to record your progress.

5. Experiment with different chunk sizes and rewards to find what works best for your particular brain.

This approach transforms the experience of time from an enemy to be fought into a series of manageable segments with built-in bright spots. It won't make time blindness disappear, but it provides a structure that accommodates it rather than being defeated by it.

Creating Routines That Stick

"Just develop better habits!"

This advice sounds reasonable, but for the ADHD brain, traditional approaches to habit formation often fail miserably. The neurotypical prescription collides with the ADHD brain's intense need for novelty and variable rewards.

Yet routines are especially important for managing ADHD time challenges. They reduce the cognitive load of decision-making, create external structure to compensate for executive function differences, and build predictability into days that might otherwise feel chaotic.

The key is developing ADHD-friendly routines that incorporate enough novelty and flexibility to keep your brain engaged while maintaining enough consistency to provide structure.

During my CPA exam studies, I gradually built a morning routine that provided crucial structure without becoming stifling. I knew I needed consistency to maximize my limited study time, but every time I tried to implement a rigid, minutely scheduled morning, I'd rebel against it after a few days.

The breakthrough came when I designed what I call a "flexible framework" routine. Instead of scheduling every minute, I created a sequence of activities with room for variation within each category:

- wake-up window (6:30-7:00 a.m.)

- physical activity (20-30 minutes of either running, yoga, or strength training—my choice each day)

- shower and dress

- breakfast + medication (with variety in what I ate)

- planning block (15 minutes to review the day's schedule and priorities)

- first focused work session (60-90 minutes)

The sequence remained consistent, but I had options within each component. I could choose different physical activities based on my energy and mood. I could vary my breakfast. The planning block might involve reviewing my planner, updating my whiteboard, or setting specific goals for the day.

This approach provided enough structure to keep me on track but enough variety to satisfy my brain's novelty needs. The consistency of the sequence helped my body and brain recognize "this is work time now," while the flexibility within components prevented the routine from becoming aversive.

I also built in what I call "routine reinforcers," small pleasures that made me actually want to follow the routine. My morning coffee was prepared exactly how I liked it. I used shower products I genuinely enjoyed. I allowed myself to listen to a favorite podcast during breakfast. These small rewards helped overcome the ADHD brain's resistance to repetition.

For evening routines, I used a similar approach but with even more flexibility. I identified the core components that needed to happen—reviewing the next day's schedule, preparing materials I'd need, and completing a wind-down sequence for better sleep—but allowed considerable variation in how and when these occurred between dinner and bedtime.

Another key element was building in recovery mechanisms for when routines inevitably broke down. Instead of an all-or-nothing mentality ("I slept through my alarm, so the whole day is ruined"), I created re-entry points ("If I slept through my alarm, my re-entry point might be something small like making my bed or brewing a cup of coffee—a quick reset that signaled the day wasn't lost") where I could jump back into my routine sequence even if I missed earlier components. This prevented the common ADHD pattern of abandoning routines entirely after small disruptions.

Perhaps most important was recognizing which areas of life truly benefited from routine and which were better served by planned variability. Morning launch sequences, transitions between activities, and evening wind-downs generally benefited from consistent routines. Creative work, physical activity, and social engagement often benefited from more flexibility and spontaneity.

Using Visual Cues and Environmental Reminders

When you're time blind, your physical environment becomes a crucial ally in managing time-related tasks. The ADHD brain typically has challenges with prospective memory, remembering to do things in the future, so embedding reminders in your environment can compensate for this difference.

During my most intensive study periods, I transformed my apartment into what my roommate jokingly called "ADHD Mission Control," a space filled with strategic visual cues that reduced my need to remember things internally.

The most obvious elements were the wall calendar and whiteboard to-do list I mentioned earlier. But I went beyond these basics to create an environment where important information was unavoidable and time was visible everywhere I looked.

I used Post-it notes strategically placed where I would encounter them at the relevant moment. Reminders to grab study materials were stuck to the inside of my apartment door. Notes about specific topics I wanted to review were attached directly to my computer monitor. The key was positioning these visual cues precisely where my attention would be when I needed the reminder, not hidden away in a planner or digital app.

Color became a powerful organizational tool. Each CPA exam section had its own color—blue for Auditing, green for Regulation, yellow for Financial Accounting, and orange for Business. All materials related to each section—folders, notebooks, flashcards, even the highlighters I used—matched these colors, creating immediate visual recognition without requiring conscious thought.

I also created what ADHD coaches call "don't-break-the-chain" visual trackers. On a large wall calendar, I'd mark each day I completed my planned study session with a bold X. As the chain of Xs grew longer, my motivation to maintain the streak increased: a powerful visual representation of consistency that appealed to my brain's reward system.

For managing specific projects, I used a simple but effective visual technique: transparent project folders positioned vertically in a desktop file holder. I could see at a glance what projects were in progress and their relative priority without having to remember to check a list or open a digital app.

Perhaps most helpful for managing time-insensitive tasks was a technique called "visual batching." Instead of trying to remember all the small tasks that needed doing eventually (returning library books, mailing forms, etc.), I created physical collection points for each category. Library books to return went in a specific bag by the door. Papers to file went in a designated tray. Forms to mail went in a special folder. When the container was full, that was my visual cue that it was time to batch process those items.

These environmental systems reduced the cognitive load of having to remember things internally and made time-related information visually unavoidable. They worked because they matched how the ADHD brain functions, struggling with prospective memory but responsive to visual cues in the environment.

Planning for Transitions and Buffer Time

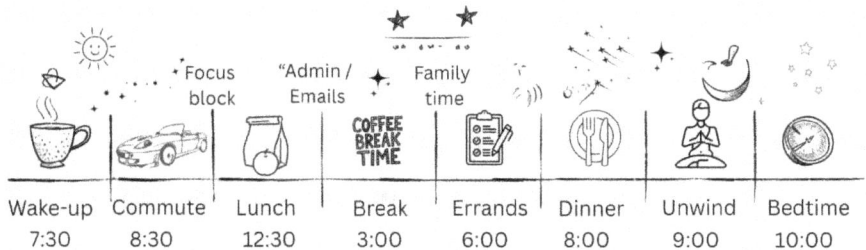

| Wake-up | Commute | Lunch | Break | Errands | Dinner | Unwind | Bedtime |
| 7:30 | 8:30 | 12:30 | 3:00 | 6:00 | 8:00 | 9:00 | 10:00 |

One of the most challenging aspects of time blindness is managing transitions between activities. The ADHD brain often struggles with task-switching, disengaging from one activity and engaging with another, which can lead to being chronically late, missing appointments, or losing large chunks of time during transitions.

I discovered this challenge during my intensive study periods. I'd schedule study sessions back-to-back, planning to switch smoothly from one subject to another. In reality, these transitions were time vortexes where minutes or even hours would disappear. I'd finish studying one topic and then get caught in a limbo of indecision, distraction, or avoidance before starting the next.

The solution came from explicitly planning for these transitions rather than pretending they didn't exist. I started building what I called "buffer blocks" into my schedule: dedicated time for the messy process of switching gears between different activities.

For example, instead of scheduling "Audit study 2-4 p.m., Regulation study 4-6 p.m.," I'd schedule "Audit study 2-3:45 p.m., Transition 3:45-4:15 p.m., Regulation study 4:15-6 p.m." This buffer time acknowledged the reality that my brain needed space to disengage from one subject and prepare for the next.

During these buffer blocks, I developed specific transition rituals that signaled to my brain that one activity was ending and another beginning:

- **Physical movement:** I'd stand up, stretch, or take a short walk to create a bodily sense of shifting gears.

- **Environment changes:** Sometimes I'd move to a different study location or rearrange my desk setup.

- **Sensory signals:** I might change the background music, lighting, or even the pen I was using.

- **Brief reset activities:** A 5-minute meditation, quick journaling, or simply closing my eyes and taking deep breaths.

These transition rituals helped create clearer boundaries between activities and reduced the likelihood of getting lost in unproductive limbo. The physical and sensory components were especially helpful for making the transition concrete in a way my time-blind brain could recognize.

I also learned to anticipate and plan for the particular challenge of disengaging from high-interest activities. When deeply engaged in something captivating (whether productive or not), the ADHD brain can experience hyperfocus.

To manage this, I set multiple alarms for important transitions, knowing I might ignore the first one. I enlisted external help, asking roommates to physically interrupt me if necessary or using apps that would temporarily freeze my computer. And I created compelling reasons to make the transition, like scheduling calls or meetings that required me to stop what I was doing.

Perhaps most important was building significant buffer time around appointments and deadlines. I learned to estimate how long something would take, then double that estimate to account for my time perception differences. If I thought it would take 30 minutes to get to an appointment, I'd allocate an hour. This reduced the constant stress of running late and missing deadlines that had plagued me for years.

Time blindness is one of the most challenging aspects of living with ADHD, but it doesn't have to control your life. By understanding your unique time perception differences and building external systems to compensate for them, you can develop a healthier relationship with time.

Key Takeaways

- **Time blindness is real:** Your ADHD brain processes time differently. The future feels abstract until it suddenly crashes down on you. This is a neurological difference that requires external systems, not more willpower.

- **Make time external and visible:** Wall calendars, visual timers, time-blocking planners, and countdown apps transform abstract time into something your brain can actually perceive. Your environment becomes your external clock.

- **Create artificial deadlines to break the procrastination cycle:** Because your brain can't feel urgency until a deadline is imminent, manufacturing earlier deadlines with real consequences helps you engage before crisis mode hits.

- **Small chunks plus frequent rewards maintain momentum:** Break projects into pieces your brain can handle, pair each completion with immediate rewards, and let the dopamine hits from small wins carry you through larger projects.

- **Build buffer time and transition rituals:** Plan for the messy reality of task-switching, create signals that help your brain shift gears between activities, and give yourself grace when time management isn't perfect.

In the next chapter, we'll explore another core challenge of the ADHD experience: emotional regulation. We'll look at why emotions often feel so intense and overwhelming with ADHD and develop strategies for riding these emotional waves without being capsized by them.

CHAPTER 4

INTEGRATE YOUR EMOTIONS

RIDING THE ADHD ROLLER COASTER

———◆○◆———

H ave you ever felt like your emotions were set to maximum volume while everyone else seemed to have access to a volume control? That's how I felt throughout much of my life, especially during the intense pressure of studying for the CPA exam. One minute I'd be confidently working through practice problems, feeling on top of the world, the next, a single difficult question would send me spiraling into doubt, frustration, and near-panic.

- "I'm never going to pass this exam."

- "Why am I so stupid? Everyone else gets this."

- "I've wasted all this time and money for nothing."

These thoughts would crash through my mind with such force that they felt absolutely real and true in the moment. My heart would race, my stomach would knot, and sometimes I'd find myself fighting back tears, all over a practice question about depreciation methods or audit procedures. The intensity felt completely out of proportion, yet I couldn't talk myself down from it.

What I didn't understand then was that this emotional roller coaster wasn't a character flaw or lack of mental toughness. It was a fundamental aspect of having an ADHD brain, one that processes emotions differently and often more intensely than neurotypical brains.

This chapter builds the "I" pillar of the *THRIVE ADHD Success Formula*. ADHD affects far more than focus and time management; it also impacts how intensely you experience emotions. Rather than trying to suppress or "fix" this emotional intensity, integration means learning to work *with* your emotions, understanding what triggers them, and developing strategies to regulate them without denying them.

Understanding Emotional Intensity in ADHD

When most people think about ADHD, they picture hyperactivity, distractibility, and trouble focusing. But for many of us living with ADHD, emotional challenges can be equally significant, sometimes even more disruptive than the attention and focus issues.

Researchers now recognize that emotional dysregulation is a core feature of ADHD, not just a side effect (Shaw et al., 2014). This isn't widely discussed in the popular understanding of ADHD, which is why so many of us spend years thinking there's something uniquely wrong with us beyond our diagnosis.

So, what's happening in the ADHD brain that creates this emotional intensity?

First, there are differences in how the limbic system, the brain's emotional center, functions in people with ADHD. This system tends to be more reactive and less regulated by the prefrontal cortex (the brain's "brake pedal" for emotions). When you experience something frustrating or upsetting, your emotional response can spike more quickly and intensely than it might for someone without ADHD.

Second, the same executive function challenges that affect focus and organization also impact emotional processing. Just as you might struggle to organize papers on your desk, your brain may struggle to organize emotional information and responses in a measured way.

Third, many people with ADHD have heightened sensitivity to rejection, criticism, and failure. This isn't just being "thin-skinned"; it's a neurologically based difference in how the brain processes social and performance feedback.

During my CPA exam preparation, this emotional intensity manifested in ways that baffled and frustrated me. I'd go from hopeful and determined one moment to despondent or irritable the next. The emotional swings were exhausting and confusing.

I remember one afternoon when I was studying audit procedures, a topic I actually enjoyed. I started the session feeling confident and engaged. Then I hit a practice problem I couldn't solve. Something about sampling methods. It wasn't even particularly difficult in retrospect, but in that moment, my inability to figure it out triggered a cascade of negative emotions.

My heart started racing. My thoughts spiraled from *I don't understand this problem* to *I'll never understand auditing* to *I'm going to fail the entire exam* to *I've wasted years of my life pursuing the wrong career.* Within minutes, I went from a confident student to someone fighting back tears over a single practice problem.

The intensity felt completely disproportionate, yet I couldn't talk myself out of it. My wife walked in and found me staring blankly at my textbook, visibly distressed.

"What's wrong?" she asked.

"I can't figure out this problem," I said, feeling simultaneously devastated and embarrassed by how upset I was.

"So take a break and come back to it later," she suggested reasonably.

Her calm response just made me feel worse; *why couldn't I react reasonably like she did? What was wrong with me that a single difficult problem could derail my entire emotional state?*

What I didn't understand then was that I was experiencing the classic emotional dysregulation of ADHD. My brain wasn't just processing the immediate frustration of a difficult problem; it was rapidly connecting that small struggle to every fear, insecurity, and past disappointment I'd ever experienced. No wonder it felt overwhelming.

It's important to distinguish between the two types of emotional challenges that often come with ADHD.

1. **Primary emotional challenges** are directly related to ADHD neurology—the intense, immediate emotional responses triggered by situations in the present moment. These include the quick flares of frustration, the sudden crashes in confidence, and the rapid mood shifts that seem to come out of nowhere.

2. **Secondary emotional challenges** develop from living with unaddressed ADHD over time. These include chronic shame, anxiety, and low self-esteem that build up after years of struggle, criticism (from self and others), and perceived failures. These become background emotional states that color everything else.

During my exam prep, I was dealing with both. The primary challenges showed up as intense reactions to daily study frustrations. The secondary challenges manifested as a persistent undercurrent of anxiety about my abilities and worth.

If any of this sounds familiar, the first step toward better emotional regulation is simply recognizing that these intense emotional responses aren't character flaws or signs of weakness. They're neurological differences that can be understood and managed, not by suppressing your emotions but by developing strategies that work with your unique brain wiring.

Recognizing Emotional Dysregulation Triggers

One of the most powerful tools for managing emotional intensity is identifying the specific situations, physical states, and thought patterns that reliably trigger your strongest emotional responses.

When I first started tracking my emotional reactions during CPA exam prep, I noticed some clear patterns emerging. Certain situations consistently sent my emotions into overdrive:

Time Pressure

Time pressure was a major trigger. When I felt rushed or behind schedule, my anxiety would spike dramatically. This was especially true when working against a timer on practice exams. The ticking clock seemed to short-circuit my ability to think clearly, creating a spiral of anxiety that made performance even worse.

Confusion

Another reliable trigger was encountering material I didn't immediately understand. Unlike some of my study partners who could calmly work through confusion, hitting a concept I didn't grasp would trigger not just academic frustration but existential dread. My brain would jump from "I don't understand this concept" to "I'm fundamentally incapable of understanding accounting" with alarming speed.

Sleep Deprivation

Sleep deprivation massively amplified my emotional reactivity. After nights of poor sleep, minor setbacks that I might have brushed off when well-rested became emotional catastrophes. A simple calculation error could trigger tears of frustration when I was exhausted.

Hunger

Hunger was another physical state that reliably triggered emotional dysregulation. I'd sometimes get so focused on studying that I'd forget to eat, then find myself irrationally angry or tearful hours later, not recognizing that low blood sugar was partly to blame.

Social Comparison

Social comparison was perhaps the most insidious trigger. Hearing classmates discuss how much they'd studied or how well they understood material would instantly trigger feelings of inadequacy and panic. Even passing comments like "That section was pretty straightforward" could send me spiraling if I hadn't found it straightforward at all.

Once I identified these triggers, I started noticing early warning signs that emotional intensity was building. Physical sensations often preceded full emotional meltdowns: a tightening in my chest, shallow breathing, tension in my jaw, or a crawling sensation under my skin. These bodily signals would appear before my conscious mind recognized that emotions were escalating.

I also noticed cognitive warning signs, specific thought patterns that signaled an emotional wave was building:

- **Black-and-white thinking:** "I either understand this completely, or I'm totally lost."

- **Catastrophizing:** "If I don't grasp this concept right now, I'll fail the entire exam."

- **Mind-reading:** "Everyone else finds this easy. They must think I'm an idiot."

- **Future-telling:** "I'll never be able to pass this exam. My entire career is ruined."

Recognizing these triggers and warning signs was the first step toward developing effective intervention strategies. Instead of being blindsided by emotional tsunamis, I could see them forming offshore and take action before they hit full force.

To identify your own emotional triggers, try keeping a simple log for a week or two. When you experience intense emotional reactions, note:

- what was happening just before the emotion hit

- your physical state (hungry, tired, etc.)

- the thoughts going through your mind

- the sensations in your body

- the emotions you experienced

- the intensity level (1-10)

Look for patterns in this data. You'll likely discover specific situations or internal states that reliably precede emotional dysregulation. This knowledge gives you power: the ability to anticipate and prepare for challenging emotional situations rather than just reacting to them after they've already overwhelmed you.

Practical Techniques for Managing Frustration and Anxiety

Once you understand your emotional triggers, the next step is developing concrete strategies for managing intense emotions when they arise. During my CPA exam preparation, I gradually built a tool kit of techniques that helped me ride emotional waves rather than being swept away by them.

The most immediately useful techniques were those I could deploy in the moment when emotions were already escalating.

Pattern Interruption

Pattern interruption became my first line of defense against emotional spirals. I learned that physically changing what I was doing could interrupt the buildup of emotional intensity. If I noticed anxiety rising during a study session, I'd immediately stand up, stretch, or even just change my seated position. This physical shift created a corresponding mental shift, giving me a moment to regain perspective.

Bathroom Breaks

Bathroom breaks became my secret emotional regulation tool. When emotions threatened to overwhelm me during group study sessions or in public settings, I'd excuse myself to the restroom. Those few minutes of privacy were invaluable. I'd splash cold water on my face, take a few deep breaths, and tell myself I was okay. That sensory reset, the shock of cold water, and a moment alone worked as a circuit breaker whenever I felt on the verge of panic or when frustration boiled over.

Grounding Technique

The 5-4-3-2-1 grounding technique became another go-to strategy. When anxiety threatened to pull me into catastrophic thinking about failing exams or ruining my career, this simple sensory awareness exercise would bring me back to the present moment:

- 5 things I can see right now

- 4 things I can touch/feel

- 3 things I can hear

- 2 things I can smell

- 1 thing I can taste

This exercise worked particularly well with my ADHD brain because it engaged multiple senses simultaneously, providing enough stimulation to capture my attention while calming my nervous system.

Structured Breathing

Structured breathing techniques provided another powerful tool. The 4-7-8 breathing pattern (inhale for 4 counts, hold for 7, exhale for 8) became my standard approach for calming physical anxiety symptoms. What made this especially effective was counting the breaths. The counting gave my active ADHD brain something to focus on while the breathing pattern itself activated the parasympathetic nervous system (the body's natural calming mechanism).

Strategic Temporary Disengagement

Strategic temporary disengagement, what some might call "taking a break," became essential when emotions threatened to derail productive study time. I learned that pushing through intense negative emotions rarely worked and often made things worse. Instead, I'd set a specific time limit for disengagement (usually 15-30 minutes), do something completely different, then return to the task. This wasn't avoidance; it was a tactical retreat that allowed me to come back stronger.

Future Memory

"Future memory" became a surprisingly effective technique for managing exam anxiety. When catastrophic thoughts about failing exams would overwhelm me, I'd close my eyes and vividly imagine myself in the future, having already passed the exam. I'd create detailed mental images of checking my passing score online, calling my parents with the good news, and celebrating with friends. This visualization not only interrupted anxiety spirals but also reconnected me with my motivation for studying in the first place.

These in-the-moment techniques were crucial for immediate emotional regulation, but I also developed longer-term strategies for greater emotional stability.

Thought Journaling

Regular journaling helped me process emotions before they reached overwhelming levels. I kept a simple notebook where I'd spend 5-10 minutes each morning and evening writing about any worries, frustrations, or anxieties related to my studies. Getting these thoughts out of my head and onto paper made them less powerful and helped me identify patterns in my emotional responses.

Scheduled Worry Time

Scheduled worry time became another effective containment strategy. I'd set aside 15 minutes each day specifically for worrying about the exam. During that time, I'd let myself consider every possible negative outcome and worry as intensely as I wanted to. But when the timer went off, I'd consciously shift to other thoughts. This contained my anxiety rather than letting it spread throughout my day.

Cognitive Reframing

Cognitive reframing, deliberately changing how I interpreted situations, took more practice but yielded powerful results. I worked on catching catastrophic thoughts ("I'll never understand this") and replacing them with more balanced alternatives ("This concept is challenging, but I've mastered difficult material before"). The key was making the alternative thoughts believable, not just positive. My ADHD brain would reject empty affirmations, but it would accept evidence-based reframing.

Physical Movement for Emotional Regulation

One of the most powerful discoveries during my CPA exam journey was how dramatically physical movement affected my emotional state. While working part-time at a metal fabrication shop during exam preparation, I noticed something unexpected:

On days when my job involved more physical activity—lifting metal parts, operating machinery, moving around—my emotional stability during evening study sessions significantly improved.

This wasn't just a coincidence. Research consistently shows that physical movement has powerful effects on the ADHD brain, including (Mehren et al., 2020):

- increasing production of dopamine and norepinephrine, the same neurotransmitters targeted by ADHD medications

- reducing levels of stress hormones like cortisol

- improving executive function, including emotional regulation

- boosting mood through endorphin release

- improving sleep quality, which further stabilizes emotions

I began deliberately incorporating more movement into my daily routine, especially during study days when I wasn't working at the fabrication shop. These weren't necessarily formal workouts (though those helped, too). Instead, I found ways to infuse movement throughout my day.

Movement Breaks

Movement breaks between study sessions became non-negotiable. After completing a practice set or reaching a natural break point, I'd take three to five minutes to do something physical: jumping jacks, push-ups, or simply walking up and down the stairs in my apartment building. These micro-workouts were brief enough not to disrupt my study flow but substantial enough to create a neurochemical shift.

Walking While Reviewing

Walking while reviewing became another effective strategy. I discovered I could review flashcards or listen to recorded study materials while walking around my neighborhood. The combination of physical movement and mental review not only helped with emotional regulation but also improved my retention of the material.

Stress Stance

Stress stance exercises provided immediate relief during moments of intense frustration. When a particular concept or problem set was making me feel like throwing my textbook across the room, I'd step away from my desk and hold a plank position, wall sit, or other isometric exercise for 30-60 seconds. The physical intensity of these exercises seemed to absorb and discharge the emotional intensity I was feeling.

Morning Exercise

Morning exercise became a cornerstone of emotional stability. On days when I could start with even 20 minutes of running, strength training, or yoga, my emotional resilience throughout the day noticeably improved. The effect was so pronounced that I began prioritizing morning movement even if it meant slightly less study time; the improved quality of that study time more than compensated for the slight reduction in quantity.

Movement Snacks

Movement snacks throughout the day helped maintain the beneficial effects. I'd do quick movements like desk push-ups, chair squats, or stretching for just one or two minutes every hour. These brief activity bursts prevented the buildup of physical tension that often accompanied long study sessions.

What made movement particularly effective for emotional regulation was its immediacy. Unlike many coping strategies that required practice and consistency before showing results, physical movement provided near-instant relief. Even five minutes of vigorous movement could shift my emotional state from overwhelmed and anxious to capable and focused.

Doodling and Fidgeting for Emotional Calm

While large-scale physical movement provided powerful emotional regulation benefits, I discovered that smaller movements, specifically doodling and fidgeting, offered their own unique advantages for emotional management.

Growing up, I was constantly reprimanded for fidgeting in class: clicking pens, bouncing my leg, and spinning pencils between my fingers. Teachers interpreted these behaviors as signs of disrespect or inattention. What none of us understood then was that these small movements were actually my brain's intuitive attempt at self-regulation.

During my CPA exam preparation, I finally gave myself permission to fidget and doodle freely without self-consciousness. The results were remarkable. Whenever I felt that twitchy, restless energy of anxiety building, having a stress ball to squeeze or a pen to click helped channel that nervous energy out of my body.

I assembled a collection of fidget tools that lived on my study desk:

- a smooth stone to roll between my fingers

- a stretchy fidget toy that could be pulled and twisted

- a silent clicking pen (considerate of others during group study)

- a small container of putty that could be squeezed and shaped

- a spinner ring that could be turned discreetly during practice exams

These items weren't distractions; they were regulation tools that helped prevent emotional tension from building to unmanageable levels. By giving my body a way to vent stress in harmless, continuous ways, I avoided the explosive release of tension that often came after trying to sit perfectly still for hours.

Doodling served a similar function but engaged my visual processing system as well. During lectures or while watching study videos, I'd keep a notepad for both notes and doodling. The act of drawing little patterns or abstract designs shifted my brain into a calmer gear, providing a bit of meditative relief without disengaging from the learning material.

What surprised me most about doodling was discovering it actually enhanced my listening comprehension rather than detracting from it. When I tried to sit perfectly still and focus only on listening, my mind would often wander completely away from the content. But when my hands were busy with simple, repetitive drawing, my ears and mind remained more fully engaged with the material being presented.

Research now confirms what I discovered through experience: For many ADHD brains, fidgeting and doodling actually improve focus and reduce stress by providing just enough additional sensory input to satisfy the brain's craving for stimulation (Sharp, 2024). This prevents the mind from seeking out more disruptive forms of stimulation (like completely tuning out or hyperfocusing on irrelevant thoughts).

If you've spent years trying to suppress these natural self-regulatory movements, allow yourself to experiment with fidgeting and doodling as legitimate emotional regulation tools. The key is finding forms that work for you without disrupting others or your own concentration on primary tasks.

Self-Compassion Practices for Combating Negative Self-Talk

Perhaps the most difficult emotional challenge during my CPA exam journey wasn't the external pressure of the exams themselves but the relentless internal critic that had taken up residence in my head. Years of struggling with undiagnosed ADHD had left me with a harsh inner voice that constantly reminded me of past failures and predicted future ones.

- "You always mess up under pressure."

- "Other people study for a few weeks and pass, what's wrong with you?"

- "You'll never be as good as the others in your program."

- "Why are you so lazy? Why can't you just focus like normal people?"

This negative self-talk created a feedback loop: The more I berated myself, the more anxious and emotionally dysregulated I became. The more dysregulated I became, the harder it was to focus and study effectively. The more I struggled to study effectively, the more evidence my inner critic had to confirm I was inadequate.

Breaking this cycle required developing a practice that felt almost unnatural at first: self-compassion. Not empty positive thinking or lowering my standards, but treating myself with the same understanding I would offer a good friend facing similar challenges.

The turning point came when I discovered research showing that self-compassion actually improves performance and resilience, especially for people facing extra challenges like ADHD (Beaton et al., 2022). This allowed me to see self-compassion not as self-indulgence but as a practical strategy for achieving my goals.

Practices to Counter Habitual Self-Criticism

I began developing specific practices to counter my habitual self-criticism.

- **The progress journal** became a powerful tool for shifting my perspective. Each evening, I'd write down three specific things I'd learned or accomplished that day, no matter how small. On particularly difficult days, these might be as basic as "I showed up to study even though I didn't want to" or "I figured out one concept I was confused about yesterday." This created a record of progress that counterbalanced my brain's tendency to focus exclusively on what wasn't working.

- **Acknowledging partial successes** represented a radical shift in my thinking. I adopted a mantra that "if I watch a lecture once and only retain 10%, that's fine; on the second round, I might get to 20%, and that's progress." This was a dramatic change from my previous all-or-nothing thinking. By rewarding myself for that 10% gain, I stayed far more upbeat and persistent.

- **The "Would you say it to a friend?" test** helped me recognize and reframe particularly harsh self-talk. When I caught myself thinking something like "You're so stupid for not understanding this," I'd ask whether I would ever say something similar to a friend struggling with the same material. The answer was always "no," which created space to find more constructive and compassionate ways to address the challenge.

- **Speaking to myself in the third person** oddly became another effective technique. Rather than thinking, "I'm so overwhelmed and behind," I'd reframe it as "Hiyasat is feeling overwhelmed right now. What does he need to help him move forward?" This slight distancing created enough space to respond more wisely to my own struggles.

- **Permission to be imperfect** in my own learning process was perhaps the most powerful shift. I realized I was holding myself to an impossible standard: expecting to learn difficult material perfectly the first time, never forget anything, and maintain unwavering focus. When I gave myself permission to learn messily, to forget things and need to review, to have fluctuating attention, to need breaks, my anxiety decreased, and my actual learning improved.

Self-compassion wasn't easy. My brain initially rejected it as making excuses or lowering standards. But over time, I came to understand that self-compassion wasn't about letting myself off the hook; it was about creating the emotional conditions under which I could actually perform at my best.

The evidence was in the results: As I became more self-compassionate, my study sessions became more productive, my retention improved, and my exam performance strengthened. Being kind to myself was more effective.

The Connection Between Physical Well-Being and Emotional Stability

One of the most surprising discoveries of my CPA journey was how dramatically physical factors affected my emotional regulation. While I'd always known there was some connection between physical and emotional health, I hadn't realized just how pronounced this relationship was with ADHD, how small changes in physical well-being could create major shifts in emotional stability.

Sleep

Sleep emerged as perhaps the single most important physical factor affecting my emotional regulation. After just one night of poor sleep, my emotional responses would become dramatically amplified—minor frustrations triggered major reactions, and my ability to self-soothe when upset practically disappeared. After two consecutive nights of inadequate sleep, my emotional state became so fragile that studying productively was nearly impossible.

I began prioritizing sleep hygiene with almost religious devotion:

- creating a consistent pre-sleep routine that signaled to my brain it was time to wind down

- eliminating screen time for at least an hour before bed

- using blackout curtains and white noise to create optimal sleeping conditions

- setting both a bedtime alarm (to remind me to start winding down) and a morning alarm

- tracking my sleep to identify patterns and issues

These changes required sacrificing some study time and social activities, but the improvement in emotional stability and cognitive function made the trade-off worthwhile. I could accomplish more in four hours of study after a good sleep than in eight hours of study while sleep-deprived.

Nutrition

Nutrition emerged as another critical factor. Through careful tracking, I discovered that my emotional stability varied dramatically based on what and when I ate. Skipping meals or relying on simple carbohydrates and sugar led to energy crashes that triggered emotional dysregulation. High-protein meals with complex carbohydrates provided more stable energy and mood.

I developed several nutrition strategies specifically for emotional regulation:

- never studying on an empty stomach

- starting each day with a protein-rich breakfast

- keeping protein-based snacks (nuts, jerky, Greek yogurt) easily accessible during study sessions

- limiting caffeine to the morning hours to prevent sleep disruption

- maintaining hydration throughout the day

Hunger, I discovered, could masquerade as anxiety or irritability. Often what felt like emotional distress was actually my body's response to needing food: a connection I'd never made before tracking these patterns.

Blood sugar stability became particularly important. When my blood sugar crashed after high-carb meals, my emotional state would crash with it. Learning to eat in ways that maintained stable blood sugar levels (protein, fat, and fiber with each meal and snack) dramatically reduced emotional volatility throughout the day.

Regular physical checkups revealed another piece of the puzzle: vitamin D deficiency was contributing to my mood instability and energy fluctuations. Supplementation, combined with more time outdoors, created noticeable improvements in my baseline emotional state.

Physical Discomforts

Perhaps most surprising was discovering how mundane physical discomforts affected my emotions. Something as simple as sitting in an uncomfortable chair or studying in a room that was too warm could significantly increase irritability and reduce frustration tolerance. Creating a physically comfortable study environment—proper chair, good lighting, comfortable temperature—was about removing physical irritants that could trigger emotional dysregulation.

This mind-body connection with ADHD appears to be bidirectional and amplified. Physical discomfort or imbalance creates more pronounced emotional effects than it might in neurotypical individuals. Conversely, emotional distress manifests more intensely in physical symptoms—tension, restlessness, and digestive issues—creating a feedback loop that can quickly escalate.

Breaking this cycle requires attending to both physical and emotional needs as equally important and interconnected aspects of brain health. The ADHD brain seems particularly sensitive to physical inputs, making basic self-care not a luxury but a necessity for emotional stability.

Emotional regulation may be one of the most challenging aspects of living with ADHD, but it's also an area where targeted strategies can create huge improvements in quality of life. By understanding the neurological basis of emotional intensity, identifying personal triggers, developing in-the-moment regulation techniques, harnessing the power of movement, practicing self-compassion, and attending to physical well-being, you can dramatically reduce the emotional suffering that often accompanies ADHD.

Key Takeaways

- **Emotional dysregulation is a core ADHD feature, not a character flaw:** Your brain's limbic system is more reactive, your executive function struggles to regulate emotions, and you may have heightened sensitivity to rejection and criticism. Understanding this neurology removes shame from the equation.

- **Identify your personal emotional triggers:** Keep a simple log of when intense emotions arise, what preceded them, and your physical state. Recognizing patterns gives you power. You can anticipate and prepare for challenging emotional situations rather than being blindsided.

- **Deploy in-the-moment regulation techniques:** Pattern interruption, grounding exercises, structured breathing, and strategic disengagement work now, when emotions are escalating. These tools don't eliminate emotions; they help you stay present rather than being swept away.

- **Physical well-being directly impacts emotional stability:** Sleep, nutrition, movement, and hydration are essential for emotional regulation. The ADHD brain is particularly sensitive to physical imbalances, making basic self-care non-negotiable.

- **Self-compassion is a practical strategy:** Being kind to yourself actually improves performance and resilience. Replace harsh self-talk with evidence-based reframing, acknowledge partial successes, and recognize that struggling doesn't mean failing.

In the next chapter, we'll explore the social dimensions of ADHD, including how to navigate relationships, manage communication challenges, and build a support network that understands and accommodates your unique brain wiring.

CHAPTER 5

VALUE YOUR STRENGTHS (WORK)

ADHD AT WORK, PRODUCTIVITY, PROCRASTINATION, AND PROFESSIONAL SUCCESS

H ave you ever noticed how different your brain feels at work compared to other settings? I certainly have. For years, I thought I just wasn't cut out for traditional work environments. Sitting at a desk for hours, managing paperwork, attending lengthy meetings where I'd struggle to stay present; it all felt like torture designed specifically for my ADHD brain.

But then something unexpected happened. When I started working at the metal fabrication shop, a job I initially took just to pay bills while studying for my CPA exam, I discovered that in the right environment, with the right strategies, my ADHD brain not only functions but actually thrives professionally.

The shop floor was busy, dynamic, and constantly changing. Problems needed creative solutions on the fly. Multiple projects moved forward simultaneously. And, perhaps most importantly, I could move my body throughout the day. To my surprise, I found myself excelling in this environment that many would consider chaotic.

This realization was transformative: The problem wasn't that I couldn't succeed professionally; it was that I needed to approach work differently than my neurotypical colleagues. When I stopped forcing my square-peg brain into round-hole work methods and instead created systems aligned with my natural tendencies, everything changed.

This chapter builds the "V" pillar of the *THRIVE ADHD Success Formula*, shifting focus from managing challenges to leveraging strengths. Your ADHD brain brings genuine advantages to professional settings: the ability to hyperfocus on interesting problems, creative problem-solving, crisis management, and the energy to push through obstacles. Rather than trying to work like neurotypical colleagues, this chapter is about creating work environments and approaches where your natural strengths shine and your challenges become manageable.

Creating ADHD-Friendly Work Environments

If there's one thing I've learned about ADHD, it's that the environment matters enormously. The right workspace can minimize our struggles and amplify our strengths, while the wrong one can leave us fighting our brains all day long.

When I became the manager at the metal fabrication shop, one of my first moves was to completely reorganize my workspace to better suit my ADHD brain. My predecessor's office was a traditional setup: desk facing the wall, fluorescent overhead lighting, and a closed door to minimize "distractions" from the shop floor. It looked like a proper manager's office, but for me, it was an environment practically designed to trigger my worst ADHD symptoms.

I completely rearranged it. First, I moved the desk to face the large window overlooking the shop floor. This wasn't just about keeping an eye on operations, though that was the explanation I gave everyone. The truth was that watching the dynamic movement of the shop provided just enough background stimulation to keep my ADHD brain engaged without pulling my attention away from administrative tasks. That constant but predictable motion in my peripheral vision actually helped me focus rather than distract me.

Next, I brought in several lamps with warm-toned bulbs to supplement the harsh fluorescent overheads. The softer lighting reduced the visual overstimulation that would often trigger restlessness and headaches by midday. I didn't have the authority to remove the fluorescents entirely, but by adding alternatives, I could at least minimize their use.

Perhaps most unconventionally, I created multiple workstations within my office for different types of tasks. My desk remained the center for computer work and paperwork, but I added a standing table for reviewing blueprints and plans, a small seating area for one-on-one conversations with staff, and even a corner with tools for small prototype work. This allowed me to match my physical environment to the type of thinking each task required and to shift locations when I felt my attention waning.

The door to my office remained open about 80% of the time—another departure from my predecessor. While conventional wisdom suggests closing your door to focus, I found that the ambient noise of the shop actually provided helpful background stimulation. Complete silence made my mind wander far more than the predictable hum of machinery and voices.

For paperwork, my greatest challenge, I created a specific ritual. I'd clear everything from my desk except the relevant documents, put on instrumental music through headphones to block unpredictable sounds, and set a visual timer where I could see it. These environmental cues signaled to my brain that it was time for focused administrative work and created boundaries around these challenging tasks.

The organization of materials was another critical factor. I used clear storage bins with large labels for supplies and reference materials, making everything visible rather than tucked away in drawers where "out of sight" quickly became "out of mind." My filing system used color coding extensively—blue folders for personnel documents, red for customer orders, yellow for inventory, and so on—creating visual cues that reduced the executive function load of finding information.

For those working in more traditional office environments, these principles can still apply with some adaptation:

- **Consider your sensory environment carefully:** Lighting, sound, temperature, and even the texture of your chair can significantly impact your focus and comfort.

- **Create zones for different types of work if possible:** Even if it's just different sides of your desk designated for different activities.

- **Maximize your visual field:** Many with ADHD focus better when they can see the activity around them rather than facing a wall or being isolated.

- **Make organization visual whenever possible:** Clear containers, color coding, and visible reminders reduce the executive function load of keeping track of materials.

- **If you're working remotely, be intentional about your home workspace:** Avoid working from bed or the couch, as these lack the environmental cues that tell your brain it's time to focus.

For many ADHD brains, a certain level of background stimulation actually improves focus. Aim to create an environment that provides consistent, predictable stimulation while minimizing unpredictable or excessive inputs that pull your attention away.

Combining Physical and Mental Activities

One of the most powerful discoveries of my working life came almost by accident. While running the fabrication shop, I found myself gravitating toward combinations of physical and mental activity whenever possible. I would often take on a physically engaging task, like welding a basic frame or sorting materials, and simultaneously listen to something mentally stimulating, like an audiobook or podcast.

At first, I felt guilty about this, assuming I wasn't giving either task my full attention. But I soon noticed something surprising: Not only was I retaining the information from what I was listening to, but the quality of my physical work improved as well. Far from being distracted, the combination seemed to help my brain find an optimal level of engagement.

I became a huge fan of self-improvement audiobooks and would listen while performing routine physical tasks around the shop. This approach kept my mind occupied and learning, preventing the restlessness that might otherwise lead to procrastination or daydreaming at work. It effectively turned my propensity for distraction into a tool for productivity.

The neurological explanation for this phenomenon makes perfect sense. Physical movement increases the production of dopamine and norepinephrine, the exact neurotransmitters that are often in short supply in the ADHD brain and that help regulate attention. By engaging in physical activity, I was essentially giving my brain the chemical boost it needed to maintain focus on mental tasks.

Physical-Mental Combinations

This discovery led me to deliberately structure my workday around physical-mental combinations whenever possible:

- Walking meetings became my standard approach for one-on-one conversations with staff. Instead of sitting in my office, we'd walk the perimeter of the shop floor while discussing projects or performance.

- For tasks requiring creative thinking, like designing custom fabrication solutions for clients, I'd deliberately use a standing desk and keep small objects to manipulate (metal samples, nuts and bolts, etc.) while sketching ideas.

- When faced with tedious paperwork, I'd pair it with subtle physical activity by using a balance ball chair that allowed continuous small movements while working.

- During inventory management, instead of delegating the physical counts to staff and just handling the numbers, I'd often participate in the actual counting and organizing while mentally tracking the implications for ordering and production planning.

- Phone calls with suppliers or clients became opportunities for movement. I'd pace the length of my office or even step outside and walk around the building during longer calls.

Ways to Incorporate Movement

Not every professional setting allows for obvious physical activity, of course. But even in traditional office environments, there are ways to incorporate movement:

- Take handwritten notes in meetings, which engages more motor activity than typing.

- Use a standing desk for portions of your day.

- Keep fidget objects in your drawer for use during phone calls or reading tasks.

- Walk to a colleague's desk instead of sending an email.

- Volunteer for tasks that include movement, like organizing the supply closet or setting up for presentations

Some tasks require visual attention that makes walking unsafe or impractical. Others may need fine motor control that's incompatible with larger movements. Through experimentation, you'll discover which combinations work best for your brain and your specific job requirements.

Managing Workplace Procrastination

Let's talk about the elephant in every ADHD adult's office: procrastination. Despite being genuinely committed to my job at the fabrication shop and finding real satisfaction in most aspects of the work, certain tasks would trigger an almost physical resistance in my brain.

The paperwork and planning tasks were my downfall: preparing the weekly schedule, writing up employee evaluations, ordering supplies, and updating the inventory database. These weren't difficult tasks intellectually; in fact, they were relatively straightforward. But they lacked the immediate engagement factor that more dynamic aspects of the job provided. So, I'd sometimes find myself pushing them to the last minute, creating unnecessary stress and rushed work.

Sound familiar? Workplace procrastination with ADHD isn't about laziness or poor work ethic; it's about how our brains respond to different types of tasks. Tasks that provide immediate feedback, involve novelty or creativity, or include social interaction tend to engage our interest naturally. But tasks that offer delayed rewards, involve repetitive steps, or require sustained attention to details often trigger our procrastination tendencies.

Strategies for Managing Workplace Procrastination

Through much trial and error, I developed several strategies specifically for managing workplace procrastination.

- **The "small chunks and rewards" approach** that had worked so well during my CPA exam studies proved equally effective at work. Instead of seeing "complete monthly inventory" as a single overwhelming task, I'd break it down into specific sections of the shop to inventory, with brief rewards between each section.

- **Pairing unengaging tasks with engaging contexts** became another powerful tool. For instance, I'd take the weekly scheduling paperwork to the local coffee shop, where the pleasant environment and background activity made the task feel less tedious.

- **Leveraging accountability through public commitments** worked wonders for deadline-sensitive tasks. I might announce to my assistant, "I'll have the schedule ready for you by 3 p.m.," which forced me to self-impose that deadline and stick to it.

- **The "just five minutes" technique** helped overcome the initial resistance to starting unpleasant tasks. I'd commit to working on employee evaluations for just five minutes, knowing I could stop after that if I wanted to. More often than not, once I'd started, the momentum would carry me forward far beyond those five minutes.

- **Body-doubling** proved surprisingly effective for administrative tasks. I'd sometimes bring paperwork to my assistant's desk and work there while they handled their own responsibilities. Their presence created a productive atmosphere that made it easier to stay on task.

- **Time blocking with buffers** became essential for recurring responsibilities. I'd schedule specific blocks in my calendar for administrative work, but crucially, I'd make these blocks 25-50% longer than I thought the task should take. This accommodated my tendency to underestimate time requirements and reduced the anxiety of feeling rushed.

- **A modified "Premack Principle"** became my go-to for particularly resistance-inducing tasks, essentially, "first ____, then ____." I'd identify something I genuinely wanted to do at work, like designing a new fabrication process or mentoring a promising employee, and make it contingent on completing the less appealing task first. "First, I'll finish the supply ordering, then I'll spend an hour on the new welding jig design."

These strategies made procrastination manageable.

Leveraging ADHD Strengths in Professional Settings

Many of the traits that used to get me in trouble, like thriving under last-minute pressure or rapidly switching focus between tasks, were actually strengths in the right context.

In the dynamic environment of the shop, being able to hyperfocus intensely when a crisis hit, like a machine breakdown or a rush order, made me the go-to person to solve problems quickly.

While my neurotypical colleagues might get flustered by the sudden change of plans or the pressure of the moment, my brain actually functioned better under those conditions. The urgency created the exact neurological conditions that helped my ADHD brain engage fully.

My knack for bouncing between many tasks meant I was great at juggling the dozens of responsibilities a manager has daily. Rather than finding it overwhelming to shift from a customer call to a fabrication problem to an employee question, I often enjoyed the challenge of handling those high-pressure moments where multiple issues needed attention simultaneously.

The "outside the box" thinking that got me in trouble in structured academic settings became a genuine asset when clients presented challenging fabrication requirements. Where others might get stuck in conventional approaches, my brain naturally generated unusual connections and creative solutions.

Even my tendency toward enthusiasm and impulsive speech had its place when properly channeled. In sales situations or when motivating the team during difficult projects, that natural energy and expressiveness helped build connections and inspire confidence.

What Strengths to Leverage and How

The key to leveraging these potential strengths was threefold:

1. recognizing which ADHD traits could be advantages in my specific role

2. creating conditions where these traits could shine

3. developing complementary systems to manage the associated challenges

What ADHD strengths might you leverage in your own professional context? Some possibilities to consider:

- Hyperfocus can produce exceptional results when directed toward complex problems requiring intense concentration.

- Divergent thinking, the ability to generate multiple solutions and make unusual connections, can drive innovation in fields that value creativity.

- Cognitive flexibility (quickly shifting between different types of tasks or thinking) can be valuable in dynamic environments requiring adaptation.

- Heightened empathy, common in many with ADHD, can strengthen client relationships and team leadership.

- Risk tolerance can be advantageous in entrepreneurial settings or roles requiring bold decisions.

- Crisis management abilities often shine in emergencies or deadline-driven work.

The goal is to find or create professional contexts where your natural tendencies become strengths rather than limitations.

Turning Hyperfocus Into a Professional Advantage

Of all the potential ADHD advantages in the workplace, hyperfocus might be the most powerful when properly harnessed. Far from being just "really good concentration," hyperfocus is a distinctive state where attention becomes so intensely locked on a specific activity that everything else (time, surroundings, even basic physical needs) seems to fade away.

At the fabrication shop, I discovered I could reliably enter hyperfocus when solving complex design challenges. One particular project stands out in my memory: A client needed a custom conveyor system with unusual angles and clearance requirements. The specifications seemed almost impossible to meet within their budget constraints.

I started sketching potential designs one afternoon, and before I knew it, the shop was closing, most staff had gone home, and I'd filled pages with increasingly refined solutions. What felt like perhaps an hour had been nearly five hours of uninterrupted, intensely productive work. The solution I developed during that hyperfocus session not only met all requirements but did so under budget, ultimately leading to a long-term contract with the client.

What made this experience different from ordinary concentration was the complete immersion in the task, the loss of time awareness, and the unusual clarity of thought. Ideas flowed with a freedom and connection that rarely happened during my normal thinking. It was as if my brain had shifted into an entirely different gear.

Through experiences like this, I began to identify the specific conditions that triggered my hyperfocus:

- complex problems with multiple interacting constraints

- visual-spatial tasks involving design or organization

- situations with clear goals but undefined methods

- contexts with minimal external interruptions

- problems that engaged my curiosity or presented a challenging puzzle

I also recognized the signs that I was entering hyperfocus:

- a subtle shift in perception where distractions seemed to fade away

- a feeling of heightened clarity and connection between ideas

- diminished awareness of physical discomfort or hunger

- a sense of flow where one thought led naturally to the next

- resistance to interruption if someone tried to engage me

Understanding these patterns allowed me to intentionally create conditions that would trigger hyperfocus for important projects.

Just as importantly, I developed systems to manage the potential downsides of hyperfocus. I set alarms to remind me of unmissable commitments. I kept high-protein snacks and water at my workstation to minimize the physical toll of extended focus periods. And I warned team members when I was entering a deep work session so they could distinguish between routine questions that could wait and genuinely urgent matters that warranted interruption.

For tasks that didn't naturally trigger my hyperfocus, I experimented with creating artificial conditions that might encourage it:

- framing routine tasks as puzzles or challenges

- setting up visual workspaces that limit peripheral distractions

- using time pressure (real or manufactured) to increase engagement

- creating physical environments that supported sustained attention

While I couldn't force hyperfocus to occur, I could significantly increase the likelihood of entering this highly productive state through intentional preparation and environmental design.

Communication Strategies for the ADHD Professional

Effective communication might be the most underrated professional skill, and unfortunately, it's an area where ADHD can present significant challenges. In my role managing the fabrication shop, I quickly discovered that my natural communication style sometimes created confusion, overwhelmed listeners, or left important details unaddressed.

My thoughts often raced ahead of my words, leading me to jump between topics or leave out crucial connecting information that existed in my head but never made it into the conversation. I'd get excited about new ideas and interrupt others before they finished speaking. Or I'd get so focused on the big picture that I'd gloss over specific details team members needed for implementation.

Communication Strategies That Work With an ADHD Mind

Through painful trial and error, I developed several communication strategies specifically designed to work with my ADHD brain.

- **Meeting preparation** became non-negotiable. Before any significant conversation, I'd take five minutes to jot down the key points I needed to cover. This wasn't a formal agenda but a personal reference to keep my communication on track. Having these points visible during the conversation helped me circle back to important items if my thoughts wandered or tangents emerged.

- **The "headline first" approach** transformed my effectiveness in giving instructions. Instead of working up to the main point through context and background (during which time I'd often lose my train of thought), I'd start with the core message or request, then provide supporting details. "We need to reconfigure the welding stations by Friday. Here's why and how I'm thinking we'll approach it."

- **Active listening tools** became essential for overcoming my tendency to formulate responses before others finished speaking. I developed the habit of taking brief notes while others talked, which not only captured their points accurately but also gave my hands something to do, making it easier to resist interrupting.

- **Visual aids** became a cornerstone of my communication approach, especially for complex or detailed information. Rather than relying solely on verbal instructions, I'd sketch diagrams, create simple charts, or even just list key points on a whiteboard. These visual references reduced misunderstandings and provided a shared focus during discussions.

- The **"three-point limit"** helped prevent overwhelming team members with too much information at once. No matter how many ideas or instructions I had, I'd force myself to group them into no more than three main points per conversation. This required prioritizing information and thoughtfully organizing my communication.

- **Developing templates** for recurring message types (project updates, order confirmations, and procedure changes) with clear sections for all necessary information was how I dealt with written communication. These templates reduced the executive function load of organizing my thoughts while ensuring I didn't omit critical details.

- **Closing communication loops** explicitly was perhaps the most important. I developed the habit of ending instructions or assignments with, "So what's your understanding of the next steps?" This simple question revealed misunderstandings immediately, rather than allowing them to surface later as mistakes or omissions.

Building Supportive Relationships With Colleagues and Supervisors

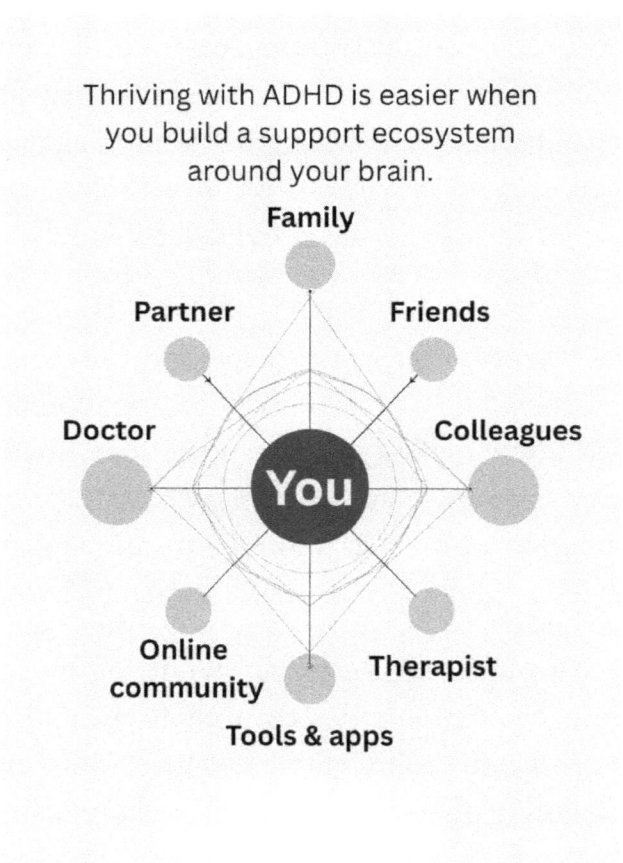

For many adults with ADHD, the interpersonal aspects of work can be as challenging as the tasks themselves. Remembering names and personal details, keeping commitments consistently, reading subtle social cues, and managing the impression we make on others are all aspects of workplace relationships that can be complicated by ADHD.

At the fabrication shop, I found myself managing a team of people with diverse personalities, communication styles, and expectations. Without deliberate strategies to support these relationships, my ADHD tendencies could easily have undermined my leadership effectiveness and team cohesion.

Strategies to Support Relationships

The relationship-building approach that proved most effective wasn't about hiding my ADHD traits but about creating systems that supported consistent, positive interactions despite those traits. Several key strategies emerged.

- **The "connection before correction" principle** transformed potentially negative interactions. When I needed to address problems or mistakes, I made a point of first acknowledging something positive about the person or expressing appreciation for their work. This small shift significantly reduced defensive responses and built goodwill even during difficult conversations.

- **Strategic self-disclosure** about my working style, without necessarily labeling it as ADHD, helped set appropriate expectations with colleagues. Statements like "I process information better visually, so I may ask you to sketch what you're describing" or "I sometimes need a moment to organize my thoughts in conversations; it doesn't mean I'm not listening" helped prevent misinterpretations of my behavior.

- **Regular one-on-one check-ins with team members** became a cornerstone of my management approach. These scheduled conversations ensured I maintained consistent contact with each person despite my tendency to get caught up in immediate problems or interesting projects. Having these meetings on my calendar with prepared talking points prevented the out-of-sight-out-of-mind problem that often affects ADHD relationships.

- **The "personal details system"** helped me remember important information about team members that might otherwise slip through my memory. I kept a simple digital note for each person with basics like family members' names, significant personal interests, and important dates. A quick review before interactions helped me maintain the personal connections that build strong working relationships.

- **Immediate follow-up on commitments** became my standard practice. When I agreed to do something for a team member, I'd create a reminder or task entry immediately rather than trusting my memory. This simple habit dramatically improved my follow-through consistency, which in turn built trust.

- **Repair strategies** for when ADHD-related mistakes affected others became an essential skill. Rather than offering vague apologies or making excuses, I developed the habit of acknowledging specific impacts, taking concrete responsibility, and proposing reasonable solutions. "I forgot our meeting yesterday, which wasted your time and delayed the project. I've now set up a better reminder system and would like to reschedule for tomorrow if that works for you."

Over time, these approaches created a work environment where my ADHD traits were less disruptive to relationships while still allowing me to be authentic rather than constantly masking. The systems and habits served as a bridge between my neurological tendencies and the legitimate needs and expectations of colleagues.

Your ADHD brain might take a different path to professional success, but different doesn't mean less effective or less valuable. With the right strategies and self-understanding, the traits that create challenges in some contexts can become your greatest professional advantages.

Key Takeaways

- **Your work environment either amplifies or suppresses your ADHD strengths:** Design your workspace around how your brain actually works: background stimulation, visual systems, movement options, and task variety. A well-designed environment can transform your productivity.

- **Combine physical and mental activities for optimal engagement:** Movement increases dopamine production. Walking meetings, standing desks, and pairing mental tasks with physical activity help your brain achieve the stimulation it needs for sustained focus.

- **Leverage hyperfocus as a superpower:** Identify conditions that trigger your hyperfocus, intentionally create those conditions for important projects, and build systems to manage the downsides (forgetting meals, losing track of time). Hyperfocus properly harnessed produces exceptional results.

- **Procrastination is about neurology, not character:** Use artificial deadlines, body-doubling, small chunks with rewards, and accountability systems to overcome the initiation resistance that comes with unengaging tasks. The goal is to make unmotivating tasks more neurologically engaging.

- **Clear communication prevents misunderstandings:** Prepare for meetings, lead with headlines, use visual aids, and close communication loops. Your ADHD communication style (rapid thoughts, tangential speaking, interrupting) can be managed through intentional strategies that work with your brain.

In the next chapter, we'll explore relationships and communication when ADHD is part of your social equation. You'll discover strategies for navigating conversations when your attention wanders, expressing your needs clearly to partners and friends, and building genuine connections without masking who you really are.

CHAPTER 6

VALUE
YOUR
STRENGTHS
(RELATIONSHIPS)

RELATIONSHIPS AND
COMMUNICATION, THRIVING
SOCIALLY WITH ADHD

———————◆O◆———————

"Are you even listening to me?"

I f you have ADHD, this question has probably been directed at you more times than you can count. You probably were listening, just not in the way the other person expected.

I can't tell you how many times I've been accused of not caring or not paying attention. My brain was fully engaged, but perhaps bouncing between the conversation, three related ideas that popped up, and the squirrel I spotted outside the window. All while genuinely caring about what the other person was saying.

Relationships are the bedrock of human existence. They're what give our lives meaning and context. But for those of us with ADHD, they can also be incredibly challenging to navigate. Our brains process social information differently, our attention ebbs and flows in ways others find confusing, and our impulse control sometimes takes a coffee break right when we need it most.

I remember sitting across from my then-girlfriend (now wife) early in our relationship as she said, "I need to know if you actually want to be with me or if I'm just this week's hyperfocus project." Ouch. But also, fair question. My enthusiasm and attention had been so intense when we first met, and then seemingly evaporated as work deadlines piled up. To her, it looked like classic hot-and-cold behavior. To me, it was just my ADHD brain shifting gears with the changing demands on my attention.

That conversation was a wake-up call. I realized that thriving in relationships with ADHD wasn't just about managing my own symptoms. It was about understanding how those symptoms affected others and finding strategies that worked for everyone involved.

This chapter continues the "V" pillar of the *THRIVE ADHD Success Formula*, applying strength-based thinking to relationships and social connection. While ADHD can create communication challenges—interrupting, inconsistent attention, time blindness affecting reliability—it also brings genuine relationship assets: spontaneity, genuine enthusiasm, creativity, and often deep empathy. This chapter is about understanding how ADHD affects your social world and developing strategies that let your authentic self show up while managing the behaviors that sometimes complicate connections.

Understanding ADHD Communication Patterns

Have you ever walked away from a conversation feeling like you were speaking a different language than everyone else? Like, there was some secret social code that everyone but you understood?

ADHD affects nearly every aspect of communication, often in ways that aren't immediately obvious to either us or the people we're talking to. The result can feel like constantly playing a game where everyone else knows the rules but you.

When I was managing the metal fabrication shop, I would sometimes interrupt others without meaning to or go off on tangents when explaining something. My mind just generated ideas rapidly, and I felt an urge to share them immediately. In meetings, I might jump in with a solution before someone had even finished describing the problem. Or I'd start explaining a concept and end up three topics away from where I began, leaving my team with confused expressions.

These weren't deliberate choices. They weren't even conscious ones most of the time. They were simply how my ADHD brain processed and responded to social information: quickly, associatively, and with limited filters between thought and speech.

One particularly memorable incident occurred during a client meeting about a complex fabrication project. The client was methodically explaining their requirements when I suddenly interrupted with, "Oh, this is just like that bridge support system we did for Henderson last year! We could adapt that design and..." I stopped mid-sentence, realizing I'd cut them off completely. The client looked irritated, and my assistant kicked me under the table. I had to apologize and ask them to continue, feeling that familiar flush of embarrassment wash over me.

How Communication Patterns Are Created

What's happening in moments like these? Several ADHD-related processes collide to create these communication patterns:

- **Working memory challenges** make it difficult to hold onto our thoughts while listening to someone else. That brilliant idea or connection feels like it might vanish if not expressed immediately, creating an almost physical pressure to speak now rather than later.

- **Time blindness** affects our perception of conversational pacing. What feels like a natural pause to us might be just a quick breath to the other person. We jump in thinking they're done, only to realize we've interrupted them mid-thought.

- **Delayed processing** paradoxically combines with impulsive responses. Sometimes we need extra time to fully process what someone has said (the delayed part), but we respond to the parts we did immediately grasp without waiting for complete comprehension (the impulsive part).

- **Attention fluctuations** mean we might miss subtle social cues that regulate conversation flow—the slight changes in facial expression, body posture, or vocal tone that signal someone is or isn't finished speaking.

- **Interest-based nervous system** makes it harder to maintain focus during conversations that don't naturally engage our interest. Our attention might drift not because we don't care about the person, but because the topic doesn't activate our dopamine systems sufficiently.

The hyperactive thought pattern leads to tangential speaking; we make connections between ideas that seem obvious to us but feel like random topic changes to others. What looks like deliberate derailing is actually our brain following its natural associative pathways.

Understanding these patterns doesn't excuse problematic communication, but it does explain it—and explanation is the first step toward change. When I finally recognized these patterns in myself, I stopped interpreting my communication missteps as character flaws ("I'm just rude" or "I'm socially clueless") and started seeing them as neurological tendencies that I could develop strategies to manage.

This shift in perspective was liberating. Instead of endless self-recrimination after social mistakes, I could focus on practical approaches to communicating more effectively. I became curious about my communication patterns rather than ashamed of them.

For instance, after realizing how often I interrupted others, I began consciously watching for it. When I caught the urge to interrupt, I'd literally bite my tongue gently, a physical reminder to wait. I also started keeping a small notepad during important conversations to jot down thoughts as they occurred. This satisfied my brain's need to capture the idea without disrupting the conversation flow.

For tangential speaking, I developed what I called my "mental roadmap" approach. Before explaining something important, I'd quickly visualize the three main points I needed to cover. This created a simple structure I could return to when I noticed myself veering off course.

These strategies didn't transform me into a perfect communicator overnight. I still interrupted sometimes. I still went off on tangents. But understanding the neurological basis for these tendencies made them manageable challenges rather than mysterious flaws. And that understanding was the foundation for all the relationship strategies that followed.

Strategies for Active Listening When Your Mind Wants to Wander

Have you ever nodded along in a conversation while your mind was actually miles away? Then suddenly panicked when you realized the other person had asked you a question and was waiting for a response?

If so, you've experienced one of the most common relationship challenges for people with ADHD: maintaining attention during conversations, especially when the topic isn't naturally engaging.

For years, I thought my solution was just to try harder to pay attention. I'd internally scold myself: "Focus! This is important!" But that approach rarely worked. In fact, it often made the situation worse by adding performance anxiety to an already difficult task.

The breakthrough came when I realized that passive listening, just sitting there trying to absorb information, is particularly difficult for the ADHD brain. We need engagement, activity, something for our brains to do besides just receiving information.

That's where active listening changed everything for me. Active listening is a practical strategy that gives your ADHD brain something concrete to do during conversations, creating the engagement needed to maintain focus.

Active Listening Techniques

At the fabrication shop, I developed several active listening techniques that dramatically improved my ability to stay present in conversations.

- **The notepad technique** became my go-to strategy for important discussions. I carried a small pocket notebook and would jot down key points or questions as others spoke. This gave my hands something to do (addressing the physical restlessness) while also creating a visual record that supported my working memory. As an added benefit, it signaled to others that I valued what they were saying enough to write it down.

- **Physical anchoring** helped when a notepad wasn't appropriate. I would maintain light physical contact with something: resting my hand on the table, holding a pen, or even just pressing my feet firmly against the floor. This subtle physical engagement helped channel restless energy and kept me grounded in the present moment.

- **The paraphrase practice** transformed both my attention and others' perception of my engagement. I made it a habit to briefly summarize what the other person had said before responding with my own thoughts: "So, what you're saying is..." or "If I understand correctly, you're concerned about..." This forced me to process their words more thoroughly while also reassuring them that I was listening, not just waiting for my turn to speak.

- **The curious questioner approach** leveraged my natural ADHD curiosity to maintain engagement. Instead of passively receiving information, I would actively look for aspects of the conversation that genuinely interested me and ask follow-up questions. This turned listening from a passive activity my brain resisted into an active investigation it enjoyed.

- **The mental visualization technique** helped with complex information. As someone explained a process or problem, I would mentally create images or diagrams of what they were describing. This visual processing engaged more of my brain and made the information more memorable.

These strategies didn't just help me listen better; they transformed how others perceived my attention and care. Before developing these techniques, I was often seen as distracted or disinterested despite my genuine desire to connect. After implementing them, colleagues and friends began to comment on how attentive I'd become.

Managing Impulsive Speech and Interruptions

My mouth has gotten me into trouble more times than I can count. Words spilling out before my brain's filter could catch them. Interrupting someone just as they were getting to their point.

Dominating conversations with excessive talking. Or suddenly changing the subject because my brain made a connection that seemed perfectly logical to me, but felt random to everyone else.

Sound familiar? Verbal impulsivity might be one of the most socially challenging aspects of adult ADHD.

During a critical client meeting at the fabrication shop, I once blurted out that their timeline was "completely unrealistic" before our sales team had a chance to negotiate. The look on our sales manager's face told me I'd just committed a serious faux pas, but by then the words were already hanging in the air. No take-backs.

These moments happen because of reduced activity in the brain regions responsible for impulse control, combined with our ADHD brains' heightened idea generation. Thoughts arise rapidly and with emotional intensity, creating an almost physical pressure to express them immediately.

Strategies to Manage Verbal Impulsivity

Through painful experience and deliberate practice, I developed several techniques to manage this verbal impulsivity:

- **The physical pause** became my first line of defense. I would literally bite my tongue gently for a few seconds when I felt the urge to interrupt. This brief physical action created just enough space for my prefrontal cortex to catch up and evaluate whether my contribution was timely and relevant.

- **The "two-breath rule"** added structure to conversation transitions. Before responding to someone's point, I would take two full breaths. This brief pause not only ensured they were finished speaking but also gave me time to organize my thoughts before responding.

- **The interruption recovery protocol** helped when prevention failed. When I did interrupt (because no system is perfect), I developed a standard recovery approach: immediately apologize, stop talking, and explicitly invite the person to continue. "I'm sorry for interrupting. Please go on with what you were saying." Simple, direct, and remarkably effective at repairing the minor social rupture.

- **The conversation contribution tally** became useful in group settings. I would mentally track how many times I'd spoken compared to others, setting a rough goal of not contributing more than my proportional share. In a meeting with five people, for instance, I'd aim to do about one-fifth of the talking. This simple awareness tool helped prevent the "dominating the conversation" pattern that can happen with ADHD.

- **The "role rehearsal" technique** beforehand was what I sometimes used for particularly important conversations. I'd mentally practice listening fully before responding, focusing on the specific verbal impulses that typically tripped me up. This preparation primed my brain to recognize and manage those impulses when they arose in the actual conversation.

As I gained better control over my verbal impulsivity, colleagues began to value my contributions more highly. When I spoke less but more strategically, people actually listened more attentively to what I had to say. My words carried greater weight precisely because there were fewer of them.

Building and Maintaining Relationships Despite Inconsistency

"Where have you been? I haven't heard from you in weeks!"

You've probably heard some version of this question from friends, family members, or romantic partners. Not because you don't care about these people, often you care deeply, but because ADHD creates patterns of inconsistency that can be confusing and hurtful to others.

I experienced this firsthand in my relationships. When I first met someone interesting, I'd be all in—calling regularly, remembering details about their lives, suggesting plans. But then, as the novelty wore off or other demands captured my attention, I'd unintentionally disappear for weeks. Not because my feelings had changed, but because my attention had shifted.

This pattern was particularly evident in my friendship with Mark, whom I met at a professional development seminar. We initially connected over a shared interest in manufacturing innovation, and for the first couple of months, we were in constant contact, exchanging articles, meeting for coffee, and calling with ideas. Then a major project consumed my attention at work, and I essentially vanished from Mark's life for nearly two months.

When we finally reconnected, he was understandably hurt. "I thought we were building a real friendship," he said, "and then you just disappeared." The pain in his voice was evident, and it made me realize how my inconsistency affected others, regardless of my intentions.

ADHD-Related Patterns That Affected Relationships

Through experiences like this, I came to understand several ADHD-related patterns that affected my relationships:

- **The hyperfocus-neglect cycle** was particularly damaging. When a relationship was new, it triggered my brain's novelty-seeking reward system, creating intense focus and engagement. But when that novelty wore off, the relationship would fall off my attention radar despite my genuine caring.

- **The out-of-sight-out-of-mind tendency** meant that people I didn't see regularly would unintentionally slip from my active awareness, not because they weren't important but because ADHD affects how recent interactions influence current attention.

- **The working memory challenges** made it difficult to retain important details about others' lives—upcoming events they'd mentioned, problems they were facing, or even birthdays and anniversaries—creating an impression of indifference despite my actual care.

- **The difficulty with transitions** affected my ability to maintain consistent communication, especially during busy periods. Shifting attention from current hyper-focus to reach out to someone required substantial executive function, which is already compromised with ADHD.

Systems That Support Relationship Consistency

Recognizing these patterns allowed me to develop systems that supported relationship consistency despite my ADHD tendencies:

- **The relationship check-in calendar** became my most valuable tool. I created a simple system where important relationships were scheduled for regular check-ins: weekly, monthly, or quarterly, depending on the relationship.

- **The personal details database** supported my challenged working memory. For close relationships, I kept notes about important events, preferences, family members' names, and current challenges they were facing. A quick review before interactions helped me maintain continuity despite memory gaps.

- **The connection ritual** established consistent touchpoints with important people. With my wife, for instance, we developed a daily "highlights and lowlights" ritual where we each shared the best and worst moments of our day. This simple practice created relationship consistency regardless of how busy or distracted either of us was.

- **The social media strategy** leveraged technology to maintain ambient awareness. While not a substitute for direct interaction, social platforms allowed me to maintain basic awareness of friends' lives during periods when my attention was captured elsewhere.

- **The radical honesty approach** transformed how I handled relationship inconsistency. Rather than making excuses or pretending I'd been consistently attentive, I began to acknowledge my patterns openly with trusted people: "My ADHD sometimes makes my attention inconsistent, but it doesn't reflect how much I value you." This transparency created space for collaborative solutions rather than hurt feelings and misinterpretations.

With Mark, I applied several of these strategies to rebuild our friendship after my disappearing act. I explained my ADHD patterns, set up regular lunch meetings in my calendar, and created specific reminders about his ongoing projects so I could ask meaningful questions.

Explaining Your ADHD to Partners, Friends, and Family

"I don't think I can do this anymore," Samira said, tears welling in her eyes. "I never know which version of you I'm going to get from day to day. It's exhausting."

We were six months into dating, and my undiagnosed, unexplained ADHD behaviors were taking their toll on our relationship. The inconsistent attention, the forgotten plans, the intense hyperfocus followed by apparent disinterest, all of it created a relationship environment that felt unpredictable and unsafe.

That conversation became a turning point. I had been diagnosed with ADHD just weeks before, but hadn't yet told Samira. I was still coming to terms with it myself and wasn't sure how to explain something I barely understood. But that night, seeing the pain my unexplained behaviors were causing, I realized that not explaining was worse than explaining imperfectly.

"There's something I need to tell you," I began. "I was recently diagnosed with ADHD, and I'm still figuring out what that means. But I think it explains a lot of what you've been experiencing with me."

That conversation wasn't perfect. I stumbled through explanations of executive function and dopamine that I only partly understood myself. But it opened a door to understanding that transformed our relationship. Samira later told me that simply knowing there was a reason behind my behaviors made them far easier to tolerate while we worked on better strategies together.

How to Explain Your ADHD

The decision of if, when, and how to explain ADHD to important people in your life is deeply personal. There's no single right approach, but I've found several principles helpful in navigating these conversations:

- **Timing matters significantly:** The best explanations happen during calm, connected moments, not in the middle of a conflict triggered by ADHD behaviors.

- **Knowledge precedes explanation:** The more clearly you understand your own ADHD patterns, the more effectively you can explain them to others.

- **Specific examples create clarity:** Rather than abstract explanations of ADHD symptoms, I found it more effective to connect the explanation directly to behaviors the person had experienced: "Remember last week when I was so focused on the project that I completely lost track of time and missed dinner? That's called hyperfocus, and it's one way ADHD affects me."

- **The distinction between explanation and excuse is crucial:** I would explicitly clarify: "I'm telling you this to help you understand why these behaviors happen, not to suggest they're okay or that I don't need to work on them. ADHD explains my challenges but doesn't remove my responsibility to manage them."

- **Collaborative framing creates partnership:** Rather than positioning ADHD as "my problem" that others must accommodate, I would frame it as a shared challenge we could approach together.

- **The level of detail should match the relationship:** Close partners generally need more comprehensive explanations than casual friends or colleagues.

- **Ongoing education supports understanding:** I found that sharing occasional articles, videos, or examples related to ADHD helped important people in my life continue to deepen their understanding over time, rather than expecting them to fully grasp it from one conversation.

- **Receptiveness varies widely:** Some people immediately understood and adjusted their expectations appropriately. Others were skeptical or dismissive, suggesting I just needed more discipline or effort. I learned to focus my energy on explaining to those who showed openness to understanding rather than trying to convince skeptics.

With Samira, that initial explanation led to a series of conversations that fundamentally changed our relationship dynamic. We developed shared strategies for managing ADHD impacts: a shared digital calendar for important events, clear communication about when I was entering hyperfocus, and explicit agreements about household responsibilities.

We eventually married, and she's now one of the people who best understands how my brain works.

Key Takeaways

- **ADHD communication patterns aren't character flaws:** They're neurological tendencies. Working memory challenges, delayed processing, rapid idea generation, and attention fluctuations create patterns (interrupting, tangential speaking, seeming distracted) that confuse others despite your genuine care.

- **Active listening requires active engagement:** Taking notes, paraphrasing, asking curious questions, and using physical anchoring give your brain something concrete to do during conversations, making it easier to stay present and showing others you're genuinely engaged.

- **Manage impulsivity through simple physical and cognitive tools:** The two-breath rule, tongue-biting, the interruption recovery protocol, and conversation contribution tallies create just enough friction to help your prefrontal cortex catch up with your impulses.

- **Systems support relationship consistency despite ADHD inconsistency:** Calendar-based check-ins, personal details databases, connection rituals, and radical honesty about your patterns help you maintain relationships despite the natural inconsistency ADHD creates. Vulnerability builds understanding.

- **Explaining your ADHD opens doors:** Sharing your ADHD patterns (at appropriate times and with appropriate people) transforms misinterpretations into understanding. Your ADHD explains behavior; it doesn't excuse it. This distinction opens collaborative problem-solving rather than resentment.

In the next chapter, we'll explore how to integrate everything we've discussed so far into a cohesive, personalized *ADHD Success System*. While individual strategies for organization, focus, environment design, and communication are valuable, their true power emerges when they work together as a unified approach tailored specifically to your needs.

CHAPTER 7

ENGAGE YOUR SUPPORT

BUILDING YOUR ADHD SUCCESS SYSTEM

———————◆◎◆———————

I used to think there was a secret to success with ADHD. Some magical approach that would finally make everything click into place. I spent years searching for that one perfect strategy, that breakthrough technique that would transform my scattered brain into a model of efficiency and focus.

There's no single secret. There's no perfect strategy.

What I eventually discovered is that success with ADHD isn't about finding the perfect solution. It's about building a personalized ecosystem of support that works specifically for your unique brain and life circumstances.

Think about it like this: If you were trying to grow a garden, you wouldn't just throw some seeds on the ground and walk away, right? You'd prepare the soil, provide water, ensure adequate sunlight, add fertilizer, protect against pests, and adjust your approach based on the specific plants you're growing and your local climate.

Your ADHD brain deserves the same level of thoughtful cultivation.

This chapter builds the "E" pillar of the *THRIVE ADHD Success Formula,* the recognition that you're not meant to do this alone. The previous pillars (mindset, attention, time, emotions, and strengths) are powerful individually, but they're most effective when used to create a coherent system supported by routines, environments, tools, and people. This final pillar integrates everything into a personalized support ecosystem.

Creating Personalized Routines That Actually Stick

"You just need more discipline."

If I had a dollar for every time someone gave me this advice about establishing routines, I could have retired years ago. The underlying assumption was always that my difficulty with consistent routines was a character flaw, a lack of willpower or commitment.

But here's what I eventually learned: The ADHD brain has a fundamentally different relationship with routines than the neurotypical brain. For us, establishing and maintaining routines isn't just a matter of decision and discipline. It's about working with our unique neurochemistry rather than constantly fighting against it.

The typical approach to routines fails spectacularly for ADHD brains. Our interest-based nervous systems simply don't generate enough dopamine to sustain attention and motivation for activities that aren't inherently engaging, no matter how important we intellectually understand them to be.

Yet paradoxically, routines are especially beneficial for ADHD brains precisely because they create external structure that reduces the constant demand on our limited executive function resources. When actions become automatic through routine, they bypass the executive function bottleneck that causes so much ADHD-related struggle.

So, how do we resolve this contradiction? How do we create routines that stick when our brains are wired to resist them?

For me, the breakthrough came when I stopped trying to force myself into conventional routine structures and started designing routines specifically for my ADHD brain. Here's what I discovered works:

1. **Anchor Routines to Existing Habits or Environmental Triggers Rather Than Specific Times:** Time-based routines are particularly challenging with ADHD because we struggle with time perception. Instead of "I'll meditate at 7:00 a.m.," I established "I'll meditate after I brush my teeth." The already-established habit (brushing teeth) became the trigger for the new habit (meditation), creating a natural flow that didn't depend on

my unreliable time awareness.

At the fabrication shop, I developed a morning "starting sequence" triggered by the physical act of unlocking my office door. The sequence was: Check the production board, review yesterday's quality reports, walk the shop floor to greet the team, then review the day's schedule. By anchoring these actions to the concrete event of unlocking the door, I bypassed my time blindness and created consistency.

2. **Build in Novelty and Variety While Maintaining the Core Structure:** My ADHD brain craves novelty, so identical routines quickly become unbearably boring. Instead of fighting this tendency, I learned to work with it by creating "routine frameworks" with variable elements.

For example, my morning routine always included physical movement, planning, and centered focus, but the specific activities within those categories could vary. Movement might be a run one day, yoga the next, or a dance party in my living room when the mood struck. The structure remained consistent while the content provided the novelty my brain needed.

3. **Use Visual Cues and External Reminders Rather Than Relying on Memory:** No matter how committed I was to a routine, my working memory challenges meant I'd often simply forget steps or even the entire routine during stressful periods. Creating visual cue cards or checklists externalized the routine from my unreliable memory.

In my home office, I posted a laminated morning routine card with checkboxes that I could mark with a dry-erase marker. This simple visual reminder became a crucial bridge during periods when my executive function was particularly compromised.

4. **Start Absurdly Small to Build Momentum and Confidence:** Every time I tried to establish an "optimal" routine all at once, I'd inevitably get overwhelmed and abandon it entirely. I learned to start with routines so simple they seemed almost ridiculous, sometimes just one or two steps, and gradually expand them as each component became more automatic.

   When establishing my evening wind-down routine, I started with just one step: putting my phone in its charging station in the living room (away from my bedroom) at 9:00 p.m. Only after that single action became consistent did I add the next step of setting out my clothes for the following day, then gradually build up to a complete evening routine.

5. **Build in Recovery Protocols for Inevitable Disruptions:** With ADHD, routine disruptions aren't a matter of if, but when. Rather than treating these as failures that derail the entire system, I learned to anticipate and plan for them by creating simple "getting back on track" procedures.

   For my workout routine, I established a three-day rule: If I missed one or two days, I simply picked up where I left off. If I missed three consecutive days, I had a specific "restart sequence" that was intentionally easier than my regular routine to lower the barrier to reentry.

6. **Celebrate and Reward Consistency Rather Than Taking It for Granted:** The ADHD brain is particularly sensitive to reward, but we often forget to acknowledge our successes with routine maintenance. I learned to build in small but meaningful rewards for sticking with routines, which helped maintain the dopamine connection necessary for sustained motivation.

   After maintaining my morning planning routine for a full month, I treated myself to the high-quality journal I'd been eyeing. The anticipation of this reward provided an extra dopamine boost during moments when my motivation was flagging.

These principles transformed my relationship with routines. Instead of seeing them as rigid prison cells that constrained my naturally free-flowing ADHD tendencies, I came to experience them as supportive scaffolding that actually created more freedom by reducing the constant executive function drain of figuring out what to do next.

The routines themselves evolved over time as my life circumstances and needs changed. The specific morning routine I used while managing the fabrication shop looked quite different from the one I developed as a consultant with a more variable schedule. The principles remained the same, but the implementation adapted to my changing life.

Environmental Design for ADHD Success

"I can't find my keys again!"

This frustrated cry was once a daily occurrence in my life. No matter how many times I lectured myself about being more organized or setting up a designated spot, my keys seemed to possess magical teleportation abilities, disappearing from where I thought I'd left them and reappearing in the most random locations: the refrigerator, a shoe, or once, memorably, in the bag of frozen peas.

What I eventually realized was that my physical environment wasn't just a backdrop for my life; it was actively working against my ADHD brain. The cluttered countertops created visual distraction, the lack of consistent systems meant nothing had a "home," and the absence of visual cues left everything dependent on my already taxed working memory.

This realization led me to one of the most transformative approaches in my ADHD management journey: intentional environmental design. Instead of trying to force my brain to adapt to my environment, I began redesigning my environment to work with my brain.

The guiding principle became simple but powerful: Your environment is your external brain. When designed thoughtfully, your physical spaces can compensate for ADHD challenges by reducing cognitive load, providing visual cues, and creating natural flows that support your functioning.

At the fabrication shop, I transformed my office from a traditional setup to an ADHD-friendly command center. I replaced the standard desk with a standing desk that allowed movement during thinking tasks. The walls became visual information centers with color-coded project boards that made priority and status immediately visible without requiring working memory. I created dedicated zones for different types of work: a computer station for digital tasks, a large table for drawings and plans, and a comfortable seating area for conversations and reading.

The transformation fundamentally changed how my brain functioned in that space. Tasks that had previously required enormous mental effort became almost effortless.

In my home, I applied similar principles with equally dramatic results. The key breakthrough was creating what I call "functional stations" for different activities, each designed to minimize executive function demands.

The entryway became a dedicated transition zone with a wall-mounted key hook positioned directly in my sightline when entering, a basket for wallet and sunglasses, and a charging station for devices, all visually obvious and requiring minimal decision-making.

The kitchen was reorganized around activity flows. Instead of storing all dishes together regardless of function, I created a coffee station with everything needed for morning coffee within arm's reach, a lunch-packing station with containers and commonly used ingredients, and a cooking zone with frequently used utensils and ingredients visibly accessible.

The bathroom counter was cleared of all nonessential items, with daily toiletries organized in a single caddy to eliminate decision fatigue in bleary morning states. Weekly medication was stored in a visible pill organizer.

My home office was designed for maximum focus with visual barriers to block distracting views, noise-canceling headphones stationed permanently at the desk, and reference materials organized by project in clear bins rather than filed away in drawers where "out of sight" inevitably became "out of mind."

Beyond these physical modifications, I discovered the power of visual cuing, using the environment itself to prompt behavior rather than relying on memory or willpower. Strategically placed objects became silent reminders that bypassed my executive function challenges:

- An open notebook and pen on the kitchen counter prompted my morning planning routine.

- A water bottle placed on my desk each morning encouraged hydration throughout the day.

- Exercise clothes laid out the night before made morning workouts more likely.

- A physical timer shaped like a tomato on my desk served as a visual reminder of the Pomodoro technique when focus was fleeting.

What works for others often doesn't work for ADHD brains. The traditional advice to "put things away" and maintain clear spaces sometimes backfired spectacularly for me. When important items were hidden in drawers or cabinets, they effectively ceased to exist for my object-permanence-challenged brain.

Instead, I developed the concept of "strategic visibility," keeping frequently needed or easily forgotten items in sight, while still maintaining overall order. Bills to be paid went into a clear wall pocket where I'd see them daily, not in a filing cabinet. Books I was currently reading stayed on the coffee table, not hidden on shelves. Project materials were stored in transparent containers labeled with both text and images.

This approach sometimes raised eyebrows from visitors accustomed to more conventional organization systems. "Why don't you put those away?" was a common question about items I intentionally kept visible. Learning to trust my ADHD brain's needs rather than conforming to neurotypical expectations was a crucial step in creating truly functional environments.

Technology Tools and Apps for ADHD Management

Let me make a confession: I'm a recovering app addict.

There was a period when I believed the next app, the next digital tool, and the next system would finally solve all my organizational challenges. My phone became a graveyard of abandoned productivity apps, each installed with enthusiasm and abandoned a week later when it failed to transform me into the organized person I aspired to be.

The problem wasn't the apps themselves; many were well-designed and genuinely useful. The problem was that I was approaching technology from a neurotypical mindset, expecting my brain to adapt to the tools rather than finding tools specifically suited to how my brain naturally works.

When I finally shifted this approach, technology became not just useful but transformative in managing my ADHD. The key was being extremely selective, choosing only tools specifically designed for or particularly well-suited to our brain patterns, and integrating them thoughtfully into my overall management system.

What Works for the ADHD Brain

Here's what I discovered works for the ADHD brain.

1. **Minimize the Number of Apps and Tools:** Each additional app creates another system to maintain, another location to check, another password to remember, and another set of notifications competing for attention. Having a small ecosystem of carefully selected tools is far more effective than dozens of specialized apps.

   My core technology system eventually consolidated to just five key tools: a single task manager (*Todoist*), a comprehensive note-taking system (*Evernote*), a calendar with robust reminders (*Google Calendar*), a time-tracking tool (*Toggl*), and a mindfulness app (*Headspace*). These five applications covered about 90% of my digital organizational needs.

2. **Prioritize Low Friction and Immediate Accessibility:** Any tool requiring multiple steps to access or use created just enough executive function demand to make consistent use unlikely. The apps that stuck were those that required minimal clicks, remembered my preferences, and made capturing information nearly effortless.

At the fabrication shop, I replaced our complex project management software with a simpler system that could be accessed with one click from any company computer. Task completion rates improved dramatically, not because the new system had better features, but because it reduced the friction of use for my brain.

3. **Leverage Visual Processing Strengths:** Many ADHD brains process visual information more effectively than text. Tools that represented information visually through colors, icons, or spatial relationships worked better for me than text-heavy lists or databases.

I used a digital Kanban board (*Trello*) for project management, allowing me to visually track task status by moving cards between columns. This visual approach made project status immediately obvious without requiring the mental effort of reading and interpreting text-based progress reports.

4. **Ensure Robust but Appropriate Notification Systems:** The right notifications can serve as crucial external reminders. But notifications that are too frequent or not actionable quickly become background noise that's either ignored or creates additional distraction.

I configured my calendar with a tiered notification system: important appointments received three reminders (day before, hour before, and 15 minutes before), while routine events received just a 15-minute warning. This matched the reminder intensity to the consequence of forgetting.

5. **Use Technology to Reduce Working Memory Demands:** The ADHD brain's limited working memory is easily overwhelmed by trying to hold multiple pieces of information simultaneously. The right digital tools can serve as external working memory, holding information reliably so your brain doesn't have to.

   Voice assistants became surprisingly helpful for this purpose. Rather than trying to remember a task until I could record it properly, I'd simply tell my phone, "Remind me to call the client tomorrow at 10 a.m.," offloading the information immediately before it could be forgotten.

6. **Embrace Automation to Reduce Executive Function Demands:** Every recurring decision or action that could be automated meant one less demand on my limited executive function resources. Technology excels at handling exactly these types of routine tasks.

   I set up automatic bill payments for regular expenses, removing the executive function burden of remembering due dates and initiating payments. Email filters automatically sorted incoming messages into action-required and reference categories, reducing the decision fatigue of processing my inbox. Recurring tasks were programmed into my task manager with appropriate intervals, eliminating the need to remember regular maintenance activities.

The specific tools and apps that work best will vary based on your particular ADHD profile, life demands, and personal preferences. What matters isn't which apps you choose, but that they truly support your brain's natural functioning rather than imposing additional cognitive burdens in the name of organization.

Building a Support Network: Coaches, Therapists, Groups, and Peers

"I should be able to handle this on my own."

This thought plagued me for years, creating a barrier between me and the support that could have made my ADHD journey easier. I saw accepting help as an admission of weakness, a confirmation that I wasn't capable enough to manage my own life.

What I eventually realized, after much unnecessary struggle, is that this perspective was fundamentally flawed. No one succeeds entirely on their own, with or without ADHD. Human beings are inherently social creatures designed to function in communities of mutual support. The myth of complete independence isn't just unrealistic; it's actively harmful, especially for those of us with neurological differences that create unique challenges.

The turning point came during a particularly difficult period at the fabrication shop. Orders were piling up, staff issues were multiplying, and my ADHD coping mechanisms were crumbling under the pressure. I was working later each night, sleeping less, and watching my productivity paradoxically decline despite putting in more hours.

In desperation, I finally reached out to James, a business mentor I'd met years earlier. Over coffee, I reluctantly admitted how much I was struggling. Instead of the judgment I feared, James shared that he'd faced similar challenges with his own attention issues and had eventually worked with an ADHD coach who transformed his approach to business management.

That conversation was the first step in building what became my most valuable ADHD resource: a diversified support network that provided expertise, accountability, understanding, and encouragement exactly when and how I needed it.

I didn't do this alone. My family's encouragement, the understanding of a few close friends and coworkers, and the wisdom of authors and experts I read or listened to, all of these were part of my support system. Through their help, I learned the importance of not isolating myself with my challenges and gradually became more confident in leveraging support tools and advocating for accommodations when needed.

What I discovered is that effective support for ADHD isn't about dependence or independence, but interdependence, creating relationships and connections that enhance everyone's functioning through mutual support. Building this network requires intentionality and sometimes courage, but the benefits are immeasurable.

Creating an Effective ADHD Support Network

Here's what I learned about creating an effective ADHD support network.

Professional Support

Professional support provides expertise and structured guidance that can accelerate progress dramatically. After my conversation with James, I found an ADHD coach who helped me develop systems specifically tailored to my unique challenges and strengths. The accountability of regular sessions kept me implementing strategies rather than just learning about them, and her expertise helped me avoid common pitfalls I would have discovered only through painful trial and error.

In addition to coaching, I eventually worked briefly with a therapist who specialized in adult ADHD. While coaching focused primarily on practical strategies, therapy helped address deeper patterns of negative self-perception and emotional regulation that had developed from years of pre-diagnosis struggles. The combination was powerful, practical tools alongside emotional healing.

Peer Support

Peer support offers understanding and normalizing that even the most knowledgeable professionals can't provide if they haven't lived the ADHD experience. I initially joined an online ADHD forum with some skepticism, unsure how strangers typing on the internet could possibly help. What I found instead was a community that immediately understood challenges I'd spent years trying to explain to others.

When I described losing hours to "time blindness" or the frustration of knowing exactly what needed to be done but still being unable to start, I received immediate recognition rather than confusion or advice to "just try harder." This validation alone was healing, but the practical tips and strategies shared from lived experience proved invaluable.

Personal Support

Personal support from family, friends, and colleagues who understand your ADHD provides day-to-day assistance that professional and peer support can't offer. This was the most challenging support category for me to develop because it required vulnerability, explaining my ADHD needs and challenges to people in my immediate life.

At work, I finally had a frank conversation with my assistant about my ADHD, explaining why I sometimes missed details in conversations or needed information presented visually. Rather than the judgment I feared, she expressed relief at understanding the patterns she'd observed, and together we developed communication approaches that worked better for both of us.

At home, my wife became my most important support person, but only after I learned to communicate clearly about my ADHD needs. We established simple support systems, she provided gentle reminders about time during social events where I'd likely lose track, and I created structure for household tasks that might otherwise be forgotten.

What made these personal support relationships work wasn't one-sided accommodation but reciprocity; I wasn't just receiving support but actively looking for ways my ADHD traits could benefit others. My creative problem-solving helped my assistant develop new approaches to persistent office challenges. My enthusiasm and energy brought more spontaneity and fun into my marriage.

The foundation of an effective support network is clear communication about your specific needs and challenges. I developed what I call my "ADHD user manual," a simple document describing how my ADHD manifests, what helps, what doesn't, and how to tell when I'm struggling. Sharing appropriate versions of this with key people in my life transformed their ability to provide effective support.

The most valuable insight I gained about support is that seeking help is a sign of wisdom. It's recognizing that none of us were meant to fight life's challenges in isolation and that leveraging appropriate support is one of the most powerful strategies available for ADHD management.

Key Takeaways

- **Routines stick when designed for ADHD brains:** Anchor routines to existing habits rather than times, build in novelty within consistent frameworks, use visual cues, start absurdly small, and create recovery protocols for inevitable disruptions. ADHD routines look different, but they work.

- **Your environment is your external brain:** Strategic visibility (keeping important items in sight), functional stations for different activities, visual cuing, and thoughtful sensory design reduce cognitive load and prevent the "out of sight, out of mind" trap that plagues ADHD management.

- **Technology amplifies capability when chosen thoughtfully:** Fewer, more targeted tools work better than many specialized apps. Prioritize low-friction access, visual representations, appropriate notifications, automation, and external working memory support. The right tools extend your brain's capabilities dramatically.

- **Support is wisdom, not weakness:** Professional coaches, therapists, peer groups, and personal relationships all serve different purposes. Building a diversified support network accelerates progress and provides the accountability, expertise, and understanding that solo efforts can't match.

- **Success with ADHD is interdependence, not independence:** The goal isn't eliminating ADHD or becoming "normal." It's building a personalized ecosystem of routines, environments, tools, and relationships that lets your unique brain function at its best while leveraging your genuine strengths.

CONCLUSION

6) Engage Your Support

5) Value Your Strengths

4) Integrate Your Emotions

3) Regulate Your Time

2) Harness Your Attention

1) Tame Your Thoughts

When I look back at that frustrated student staring at the same paragraph over and over, I hardly recognize him. Not because I've conquered ADHD; it's still very much a part of who I am. But because I've turned down the negative noise of self-doubt and disorganization and amplified my unique voice in the professional world.

Remember that fabrication shop where I once struggled to keep track of projects and deadlines? By my final year there, I was leading the team in developing innovative solutions for our most challenging clients. The same divergent thinking that made linear tasks so difficult allowed me to see connections and possibilities others missed entirely. My ability to hyperfocus during critical design phases produced breakthroughs that became company signatures. Even writing this book, transforming scattered thoughts into coherent chapters that might help others, stems directly from my ADHD-driven resilience and intense focus on topics that genuinely matter to me.

These weren't accomplishments that happened despite my ADHD. They happened, in many ways, because of it.

The journey hasn't been a straight line. There are still days when I lose my keys, miss appointments, or find myself deep in an unplanned research rabbit hole when a deadline looms. ADHD hasn't disappeared from my life, and it never will. But its power to derail my days, damage my relationships, and diminish my self-worth has dramatically decreased as I've built systems that work with my brain rather than against it.

What's changed deeply is my relationship with my own mind. Where I once saw only disorder and deficiency, I now recognize a different, not lesser, way of processing the world. I've stopped trying to force my square-peg brain into society's round holes and instead created spaces and approaches that actually fit how I function.

This shift hasn't happened through wishful thinking or empty self-affirmation. It's been built through concrete, practical steps—developing personalized routines, designing supportive environments, leveraging helpful technologies, building genuine support networks, and integrating these elements into a coherent system that works specifically for my unique brain. It's been built through compassionate persistence, getting back up after inevitable setbacks and adjusting approaches rather than abandoning them entirely.

Having ADHD doesn't doom you to chaos or failure. It's all about understanding yourself and finding what tools and environment you need to shine. If you're willing to put in the work, to seek out what helps you focus, to structure your time in ways that suit you, to care for your emotional health, to communicate openly, and to ask for support, you can change your world. What used to be daily struggles can become your superpowers.

The transformation isn't about becoming someone else or somehow eliminating your ADHD. It's about becoming more effectively yourself, working with your natural brain wiring rather than constantly fighting against it, leveraging your unique strengths while appropriately supporting your challenges.

Your journey won't look exactly like mine, but I hope the road is now a little clearer because we've walked part of it together. Maybe the routine frameworks that revolutionized my mornings will need significant modification to fit your life circumstances. Perhaps the environmental design principles that transformed my workspace will take different forms in your home or office. The technology tools that extended my capabilities might be replaced by completely different resources that better match your specific needs.

That's exactly as it should be. *The ADHD Success Formula* isn't a rigid prescription; it's an invitation to discover your own unique formula for turning different into remarkable. Take what works, adapt what needs changing, and leave what doesn't serve you.

If there's one thing I hope you take from these pages, it's this: Your differently wired brain has value precisely because it's different. We need diverse thinking more than ever. The very traits that have sometimes made conventional paths challenging are increasingly valuable in solving the complex problems we face.

Your ADHD brain isn't broken. It's specialized. Your challenge isn't to fix it, but to find where and how it shines brightest, then build the supports that allow that brilliance to emerge consistently. When you do, you won't just manage ADHD, you'll transform it from an obstacle into a remarkable advantage.

If this book has supported you, encouraged you, or helped you understand yourself a little better, I'd be truly grateful if you could take a moment to leave a review. Your feedback not only helps other readers find the guidance they may be searching for, but it also allows this work to reach and support more people on their own ADHD journeys. Thank you for being part of this one.

GLOSSARY

- **Active Listening:** Fully concentrating on what someone is saying rather than passively hearing their words.

- **Body-Doubling:** The practice of having another person work alongside you (in person or virtually) to help maintain focus and productivity.

- **Decision Fatigue:** The deterioration of decision-making quality after making many consecutive decisions.

- **Divergent Thinking:** The thought process of generating creative ideas by exploring many possible solutions.

- **Dopamine:** A neurotransmitter involved in motivation, reward, and attention.

- **Executive Functions:** Higher-order cognitive processes that include working memory, flexible thinking, and self-control.

- **External Scaffolding:** Physical or digital systems that provide structure and support for areas where executive functioning may be weak.

- **Hyperfocus:** An intense state of concentration that can last for extended periods when engaged in stimulating or interesting activities.

- **Impulsivity:** Acting without forethought or consideration of consequences.

- **Interest-Based Nervous System:** The concept that ADHD brains are motivated by interest, challenge, and novelty rather than importance or obligation.

- **Neurodivergent:** Having a brain that functions differently from the societal standard; includes ADHD, autism, dyslexia, and other conditions.

- **Pomodoro Technique:** A time management method using alternating work periods (typically 25 minutes) and short breaks to maintain focus and productivity.

- **Prioritization Matrix:** A tool for ranking tasks based on importance and urgency to help decision-making when overwhelmed.

- **Procrastivity:** Being busy with less important tasks to avoid more important but challenging ones.

- **Sensory Processing:** How the nervous system receives and responds to sensory information.

- **Time Blindness:** Difficulty perceiving or estimating the passage of time, leading to chronic lateness or poor time management.

- **Time Blocking:** A scheduling technique where specific time periods are dedicated to particular tasks or categories of work.

- **Visual Cues:** Physical reminders (like sticky notes or color-coding) that help prompt memory and action.

- **Working Memory:** The mental workspace where information is temporarily held and manipulated.

REFERENCES

Adesman, A. R. (2001). The diagnosis and management of attention-deficit/hyperactivity disorder in pediatric patients. *The Primary Care Companion to the Journal of Clinical Psychiatry*, *03*(02), 66–77. https://doi.org/10.4088/pcc.v03n0204

Beaton, D. M., Sirois, F., & Milne, E. (2022). The role of self-compassion in the mental health of adults with ADHD. *Journal of Clinical Psychology*, *78*(12). https://doi.org/10.1002/jclp.23354

Costanzo, F., Fucà, E., Menghini, D., Circelli, A. R., Carlesimo, G. A., Costa, A., & Vicari, S. (2021). Event-Based prospective memory deficit in children with ADHD: Underlying cognitive factors and association with symptoms. *International Journal of Environmental Research and Public Health*, *18*(11), 5849. https://doi.org/10.3390/ijerph18115849

Curatolo, P., D'Agati, E., & Moavero, R. (2010). The neurobiological basis of ADHD. *Italian Journal of Pediatrics*, *36*(1), 79. https://doi.org/10.1186/1824-7288-36-79

Ford, T. (2020). Transitional care for young adults with ADHD: transforming potential upheaval into smooth progression. *Epidemiology and Psychiatric Sciences*, *29*. https://doi.org/10.1017/s2045796019000817

Frick, M. A., Brandt, A., Hellund, S., & Grimell, J. (2025). ADHD and identity formation: Adolescents' experiences from the healthcare system and peer relationships. *Journal of Attention Disorders*, *29*(7). https://doi.org/10.1177/10870547251318484

Ginapp, C. M., Greenberg, N. R., MacDonald-Gagnon, G., Angarita, G. A., Bold, K. W., & Potenza, M. N. (2023). The experiences of adults with ADHD in interpersonal relationships and online communities: A qualitative study. *SSM - Qualitative Research in Health*, *3*(100223), 100223. https://doi.org/10.1016/j.ssmqr.2023.100223

Green, R. (2024, July 22). *ADHD symptom spotlight: Interrupting.* Verywell Mind. https://www.verywellmind.com/adhd-symptom-spotlight-interrupting-6256766

Hallowell, E. (2020, January 29). *Changing your perspective on ADHD.* Dr. Hallowell. https://drhallowell.com/2020/01/29/changing-your-perspective-on-adhd/

Low, K. (2023, March 3). *The relationship between ADHD and chronic procrastination.* Verywell Mind. https://www.verywellmind.com/adhd-and-chronic-procrastination-20379

Mandolesi, L., Polverino, A., Montuori, S., Foti, F., Ferraioli, G., Sorrentino, P., & Sorrentino, G. (2018). Effects of physical exercise on cognitive functioning and wellbeing: Biological and psychological benefits. *Frontiers in Psychology*, *9*(9). https://doi.org/10.3389/fpsyg.2018.00509

Martín-Rodríguez, A., Herrero-Roldán, S., & Clemente-Suárez, V. J. (2025). The role of physical activity in

ADHD management: Diagnostic, digital, and non-digital interventions, and lifespan considerations. *Children*, *12*(3), 338. https://doi.org/10.3390/children12030338

Mehren, A., Reichert, M., Coghill, D., Müller, H. H. O., Braun, N., & Philipsen, A. (2020). Physical exercise in attention deficit hyperactivity disorder – evidence and implications for the treatment of borderline personality disorder. *Borderline Personality Disorder and Emotion Dysregulation*, *7*(1). https://doi.org/10.1186/s40479-019-0115-2

Nall, R. (2012). *The upside of ADHD: Leadership, athleticism, creativity, hyperfocus*. Healthline. https://www.healthline.com/health/adhd/benefits-of-adhd

Parsamanesh, P., & Vysochyn, M. (2024). A psychological exploration of the power of our mindset and its influence on physiological health. *Cureus*, *16*(1). https://doi.org/10.7759/cureus.52505

Pistoia, Jared. C. (2023, June 9). *ADHD and speech problems: What's the connection?* Healthline. https://www.healthline.com/health/adhd/adhd-and-speech

Rubia, K. (2018). Cognitive neuroscience of attention deficit hyperactivity disorder (ADHD) and its clinical translation. *Frontiers in Human Neuroscience*, *12*(100). https://doi.org/10.3389/fnhum.2018.00100

Saline, S. (2025, May 9). *5 reasons routines fizzle – and how to rekindle healthy habits*. AdditudeMag. https://www.additudemag.com/how-to-stick-to-a-routine-adhd/

7 myths (and the facts) about ADHD. (2024, May 13). Cleveland Clinic. https://health.clevelandclinic.org/myths-about-adhd

Sharp, M. R. (2024, October 30). *Does fidgeting help people with ADHD focus?* UC Davis Health.

https://health.ucdavis.edu/news/headlines/does-fidgeting-help
-people-with-adhd-focus-/2024/10

Shaw, P., Stringaris, A., Nigg, J., & Leibenluft, E. (2014). Emotion dysregulation in attention deficit hyperactivity disorder. *American Journal of Psychiatry*, *171*(3), 276–293. https://doi.org/10.1176/appi.ajp.2013.13070966

Sherrell, Z. (2021, July 21). *6 strengths and benefits of ADHD*. MedicalNewsToday. https://www.medicalnewstoday.com/articles/adhd-benefits

Söderlund, G., Sikström, S., & Smart, A. (2007). Listen to the noise: Noise is beneficial for cognitive performance in ADHD. *Journal of Child Psychology and Psychiatry*, *48*(8), 840–847. https://doi.org/10.1111/j.1469-7610.2007.01749.x

Weissenberger, S., Schonova, K., Büttiker, P., Fazio, R., Vnukova, M., Stefano, G. B., & Ptacek, R. (2021). Time perception is a focal symptom of attention-deficit/hyperactivity disorder in adults. *Medical Science Monitor*, *27*. https://doi.org/10.12659/msm.933766

What are people with ADHD good at? (2024, November 20). Oxford CBT. https://www.oxfordcbt.co.uk/what-are-people-with-adhd-good-at/

www.ingramcontent.com/pod-product-compliance
Lightning Source LLC
Chambersburg PA
CBHW051622120626
46551CB00014B/1904